METHODS AND TOOLS
FOR SOFTWARE
CONFIGURATION
MANAGEMENT

WILEY SERIES IN SOFTWARE ENGINEERING PRACTICE

Series Editors:

Patrick A.V. Hall, *The Open University, UK*
Martyn A. Ould, *Praxis Systems plc, UK*
William E. Riddle, *Software Design & Analysis, Inc., USA*

METHODS AND TOOLS FOR SOFTWARE CONFIGURATION MANAGEMENT

David Whitgift
Logica plc, UK

JOHN WILEY & SONS
Chichester • New York • Brisbane • Toronto • Singapore

Other Wiley Editorial Offices

John Wiley & Sons, Inc., 605 Third Avenue,
New York, NY 10158-0012, USA

Jacaranda Wiley Ltd, G.P.O. Box 859, Brisbane,
Queensland 4001, Australia

John Wiley & Sons (Canada) Ltd, 5353 Dundas Street West,
Fourth Floor, Etobicoke, Ontario M9B 6H8, Canada

John Wiley & Sons (SEA) Pte Ltd, 37 Jalan Pemimpin 05-04,
Block B, Union Industrial Building, Singapore 2057

Library of Congress Cataloging-in-Publication Data:

Whitgift, David.
    Methods and tools for software configuration management / David
Whitgift.
        p.   cm.—(Wiley series in software engineering practice)
    Includes bibliographical references and index.
    ISBN 0 471 92940 9
    1. Software configuration management. I. Title. II. Series.
QA76.76.C69W55   1991
005.1—dc20   91–23191
                                                              CIP

A catalogue record for this book is available from the British Library

Printed and bound in Great Britain by
Biddles Ltd, Guildford and King's Lynn

To Jane

CONTENTS

PREFACE

This book is about the Configuration Management (CM) of software: a collection of techniques which identify and control changes to software being developed by a team of programmers. The book aims to describe CM in a way which is both pragmatic and theoretically sound. Its objectives are to:

- Introduce the *concepts* of CM and a precise language for talking about these concepts. The concepts provide the framework for the rest of the book. The language includes terms like item, version, variant, configuration and dependency; all the terms are collected in a glossary.

- Describe the *principles* of CM. Although different software projects have different CM requirements, there are many tried and proven CM principles which apply to all projects. The areas which these principles address include software structuring, CM procedures, planning and the use of software tools.

- Show how to put the principles of CM into *practice*. All the principles of CM are illustrated by examples; many of these examples are brief, others are extended case studies.

Chapter 1 includes a summary of each chapter of the book. Every chapter except the first concludes with a list of key points from the chapter. The book will be of interest to anyone concerned with developing and maintaining software, including computer programmers, team leaders, project managers and consultants. The reader is not assumed to have any knowledge of particular programming languages, design methods, operating systems or software tools. In theory the book could be read by a student at the beginning of a degree course in computer science. In practice the readers who will benefit most from the book will have had some experience developing or maintaining software as part of a team.

The book contains a few fragments of code written in C and Ada which illustrate aspects of CM; the details of the code are not important and can be ignored without significant loss. There are also some examples of very simple commands which compile and link a program. The syntax of these commands is not that of any operating system, but the meaning of the commands is either self explanatory or is explained in the text.

Last but not least, it is a pleasure to acknowledge and thank Rosemary Altoft (John Wiley and Sons), Susan Dart (Software Engineering Institute), Pat Hall (The Open University), John Lambert (Rational), Alex Lobba (Softool Corporation), Alastair Tilbury (Yard Software Systems) and Jane Whitgift for their help and advice. Thanks also to the management of Logica Cambridge for their support.

D. Whitgift

1

INTRODUCTION

Configuration Management (CM) is a collection of techniques which coordinate and control the construction of a system. Engineers have been developing complex systems for millennia. Many of the principles of CM were developed to enable hardware engineers design and assemble the components of ever more sophisticated configurations. Some of the principles would have been familiar to the project manager charged with building the pyramids.

In the 1990s millions of men and women develop complex systems using software. These systems consist of a myriad of component parts each of which evolves as it is developed and maintained. Software CM ensures that this evolution is efficient and controlled, so that the individual components fit together to form a coherent whole.

Using software to build systems is both a challenge and an opportunity for CM—a challenge because software is so notoriously easy to change (the rate of evolution of a large software system strains to the limit the CM techniques which were designed to manage hardware) and an opportunity because the use of software allows CM to be automated (by its nature, software can be stored by a computer). Software tools which automate CM are able to take on much of the responsibility for the safe custody of software and for controlling its evolution.

In the context of CM a component of a system is called a *configuration item*, or more briefly an *item*. An item is a part of the system which is treated as a unit for the purposes of CM. The range of items which software CM must manage is very wide and includes source code, executable code, user and system documentation, test data, support software, libraries, specifications and project plans. An item of source code may be an Ada package, a SQL query or a screen layout which has been defined with an interactive tool. From the perspective of CM the detailed content of an item is of secondary importance. CM is more concerned with the relationships between items; for

1

example, that one item is derived from another using a software tool like a compiler or that a large item such as a subsystem is composed of other items. Knowledge of the relationships between items allows CM procedures to be formalised and automated.

1.1 THE PROBLEM

Anyone who has worked as part of a team developing software will be aware of the problems of coordination and control. The list that follows is a cross section of the questions that often arise during the development and maintenance of a large software system. [Tichy 88] highlights a similar set of questions.

1.1.1 Version management

In an ideal world only one version of each item would be needed. In practice versions of an item are needed to correct errors and to meet different requirements. As the system evolves versions of its constituent items multiply. Version management provides answers to questions like:

- How should the system be structured so that different systems can be built to meet the requirements of different users?

- How should an old version of the system be preserved, for example, to investigate a fault?

- How can a version of the system be built so that it contains certain fixes but not others?

- How may two engineers work on the same item at the same time?

- How can many versions of an item be stored efficiently?

1.1.2 Item identification

Engineers must be able to identify the items which they are developing or maintaining. In particular, each item must have a unique name and the name must be qualified with the version of the item. Item identification addresses concerns such as:

- Is this the same system in which the fault has been reported?

- What are the constituent items of this system?

- The system worked yesterday; what has changed?
- Why is the behaviour of this item not consistent with this listing?
- What is the status of this item—has it been tested?
- How did this item evolve to its present state?

1.1.3 Building the system

Assembling a software system usually involves using tools to transform the source items produced by engineers into executable programs. Compilers and linkers are typical examples of such tools. Effective control of the way in which the system is built provides answers to questions like:

- What source code and compiler options should be used to build the system?
- How much of the system needs to be recompiled after one item has been changed?
- Were there any compilation errors or warnings when the system was built?
- What is the right order to perform the steps which build the system?
- What are the implications of installing a new version of the compiler?

1.1.4 Change control

Changes to items which have been approved, for example following testing or formal review, must be carefully controlled if engineers are to work together productively. The strictness of the change control for an item needs to increase with the extent to which other items depend upon it. Change control addresses issues such as:

- What is the correct procedure for proposing, evaluating and implementing a change?
- What will be the impact of a proposed change?
- Which faults are fixed in this version of the system and which are outstanding?
- Has everyone with an interest in this item been informed that it has changed?

- Has a change been properly tested?
- Are there any changes planned for this item?

1.1.5 Library management

All software which is important to a project must be configuration managed as items. The library of items must therefore be stored securely and reliably. Good library management provides answers to the following questions:

- When should backup copies of items be made to insure against their loss or corruption?
- The disk containing the library crashes—how does the project recover using backups?
- When should items be archived to secondary storage?
- How is unauthorised access to items prevented?
- When and how should the system be released to users?

1.2 AN OVERVIEW OF THE SOLUTION

The discipline of CM addresses precisely the problems described in the previous section. According to [Babich 86], 'CM is the art of identifying and controlling modifications to the software being built by a programming team'. A more formal definition of CM is given by [IEEE-729 83]: 'CM is the process of identifying and defining the items in the system, controlling the change of these items throughout their lifecycle, recording and reporting the status of items and change requests, and verifying the completeness and correctness of items'.

Although these two definitions are consistent, they emphasise different aspects of CM. Babich's definition emphasises the role of CM in technical management and the benefits it provides to a team of programmers. The IEEE definition emphasises the project management aspects of CM, for example change control. The definitions highlight a spectrum of concerns for CM. At one end of the spectrum, programmers make frequent changes to fragments of untested code. At the other end, configuration control boards review a few changes to items which have been highly approved. To be effective CM must address both ends of this spectrum.

Following this introduction, Chapter 2 discusses the context in which CM operates: the project lifecycle. In the 1960s and 1970s most projects, if they were well managed, followed some form of the waterfall model and it was sensible to discuss CM in that context. Today there are more flexible and powerful lifecycle models which encompass evolutionary development, prototyping and incremental development. These models require the more general approach to CM which is outlined in this chapter.

Chapter 3 classifies items and the relationships between them. The two most important relationships between items are decomposition and dependency. The decomposition relationship, which arises when one item is a part of another, leads to the concept of the design item hierarchy. The dependency relationship arises when a change to one item might require a change to another. The need to minimise dependencies is an important guideline for structuring the design item hierarchy which leads to the concepts of interfaces and information hiding. This chapter also introduces the key distinction between source items and derived items.

Chapter 4 solves the version management problems listed in Section 1.1. The chapter describes how an item is either mutable or controlled, and that the only way to change a controlled item is to create a new version of the item. A version of an item which is intended to be an improvement upon its predecessor is called a revision. Versions which allow one item to meet conflicting requirements at the same time are called variants; for example, variants of an item may be needed for different operating system platforms. This chapter describes a range of methods and tools for managing variance, which is one of the central problems of CM.

Chapter 5 solves the item identification problems listed in Section 1.1. The assumption is that items are structured according to the principles of Chapter 3. Identification of a version of an item involves naming the item, specifying its version, describing how the item was constructed and describing its basic properties. The identification of the item must be recorded visibly and reliably so that there is no difficulty or uncertainty in answering the question, 'What item is this?'. This chapter describes the different methods and tools which are appropriate for identifying source items, derived items and configurations.

Chapters 6, 7 and 8 all describe methods and tools for defining and building configurations. Chapter 6 first summarises the principles which underly all approaches to the problem: a system model which describes the relationships between the items in the configuration, a mechanism for selecting the required item versions, and a way of reusing existing derived items. Chapter 6 goes on to describe how to put these principles into practice using the basic facilities which are provided by most operating systems. The chapter concludes by describing how configurations can be built efficiently using Make or a similar tool. Chapters 7 and 8 describe more sophisticated methods and tools for defining and building configurations. Chapter 7 is a detailed description of DSEE, which is one of the best CM tools in widespread use; the chapter concludes with a case study which illustrates the practical use of DSEE. Chapter 8 discusses the particular CM requirements of Ada and describes how these requirements are met by the Rational Environment. Neither of Chapters 7 or 8 is essential to the rest of the book.

Chapters 9 and 10 solve the change control problems listed in Section 1.1. Chapter 9 describes the principles of change control and how the principles may be put into practice using manual (i.e. paper-based) approaches. The principles are described in terms of the lifecycle of an item version, the lifecycle of a request for change and the role of the configuration control board in coordinating these lifecycles. The chapter provides several examples of proformas which may be used to request and control change; it also suggests how these proformas may be adapted to meet the needs of a particular project. Chapter 10 shows how the practice of change control can be improved by using CM tools. Four specific tools are described: MRCS, Lifespan, CCC and PCMS. Each of these tools has strengths which illustrate important aspects of change control. Chapter 10 is not essential to the rest of the book.

Chapter 11 solves the problems of library management listed in Section 1.1. It describes strategies for archive, backup and access control which improve the security and integrity of the library. It also describes when and how configurations should be released from the library to users. The rest of Chapter 11 discusses the integration of a CM tool with other software tools. Every tool produces software which must be managed as an item, so the software library should be the linchpin which integrates all the tools in the environment. Unfortunately this integration of data is hard to achieve in practice. The chapter concludes with a discussion of future trends for data integration which includes brief descriptions of PCTE and IRDS.

Chapter 12 brings together all the threads of the previous chapters. It describes how to plan CM, it suggests when to do what, it highlights common pitfalls and it proposes remedial action if things go wrong. Every project is different so this chapter is closer to a checklist than to a cookbook. The topics covered include how to structure and when to write a CM plan, how to organise a project team to ensure effective CM, how to select a suitable CM tool and how to introduce good CM practice to an organisation.

In the course of the book, five principles become apparent which are the keys to effective CM. They are that CM should be:

- *Proactive.* CM should be viewed not so much as a solution to the problems listed in the previous section but as a collection of procedures which ensure that the problems do not arise. All too often CM procedures are instituted in response to problems rather than to forestall them. CM must be carefully planned.

- *Flexible.* CM controls must be sensitive to the context in which they operate. Within a single project an element of code which is under development should not be subject to restrictive change control; once it has been tested and approved change control needs to be formalised. Different projects may have very different CM requirements.

- *Automated.* All aspects of CM can benefit from the use of software tools; for some aspects, CM tools are all but essential. Much of this book is concerned with describing how CM tools help. Beware, however, that no CM tool is a panacea for all CM problems.

- *Integrated.* CM should not be an administrative overhead with which engineers periodically have to contend. CM should be the linchpin which integrates everything an engineer does; it provides much more than a repository where completed items are deposited. Only if an engineer attempts to subvert CM controls should he or she be conscious of the restrictions which CM imposes.

- *Visible.* Many of the issues raised in the previous section stem from ignorance of the content of items, the relationships between items and the way items change. CM requires that any activity which affects items should be conducted according to clearly defined procedures which leave a visible and auditable record of the activity.

1.3 THE BOUNDS OF CM

Sadly CM is not the answer to all the problems and pitfalls that can afflict software development and maintenance! CM does not provide a design method or lifecycle model, it does not estimate the commercial risks associated with a project, nor define how the quality of items is to be judged. It does, however, provide a solid foundation for all other software engineering activities.

CM is particularly closely related to two other quality control activities: testing and project management. CM defines at what stage of its evolution an item should be tested or reviewed, as well as the effect of the result of the test on how the item is subsequently managed. CM does not address how testing should be conducted; this book does not describe formal reviews, inspections, walkthroughs or dynamic testing techniques.

Part of planning a project is to divide the work that must be done into workpackages; this division will, and should, closely resemble the way in which the system to be built is divided into items. This book draws attention to these sorts of relationships between CM and project management, but it does not describe classic tools of project management such as Gantt charts, cost estimation models and critical path analysis. See [Ould 90] for a very readable introduction to project and quality management.

1.4 THE BENEFITS

The history of the software industry is strewn with well-publicised failures. Who knows how many more such failures have been covered up, an embarrassment to those responsible for them? Many of these failures are attributable to the absence of CM. Other quality control activities are simply not possible without CM as a foundation.

The vital importance of CM is being increasingly recognised. Standards organisations are prescribing CM procedures and are requiring that the procedures be supported by CM tools. The suppliers of CASE (Computer Aided Software Engineering) tools which obstruct even rudimentary CM are responding to the anguished cries of their users that the tool is unsuitable for all but the smallest project. The developers of software engineering environments are recognising the central role of CM.

The discipline of CM described in this book addresses all the problems listed in Section 1.1. Solutions to these problems provide two important and distinct benefits. The obvious benefit is that the quality of the delivered software product is improved and the cost of developing and maintaining it is reduced. The second benefit is to the morale of software engineers. Working in a poorly managed environment can be a deeply dispiriting experience. CM allows engineers to do what they should be doing and what they enjoy doing: designing, developing and maintaining software.

2

CONFIGURATION MANAGEMENT AND THE PROJECT LIFECYCLE

This chapter describes the context in which CM operates: the project lifecycle. Over the last thirty years, engineers have used many different models for the project lifecycle. The first two sections of this chapter, which are strongly influenced by [Boehm 86], summarise the most successful lifecycles for software development. The third section discusses the impact of different lifecycles upon CM. The last section describes CM during the maintenance phase of a project.

2.1 THE WATERFALL MODEL AND ITS PRECURSORS

When programming was in its infancy, the tasks a programmer undertook were of two and only two kinds: coding and debugging. The limitation of this approach was that it failed to recognise the importance of designing something before building it. It did not provide models of the program which could be used both to confirm that the program would be fit for its intended purpose and to define a practical and maintainable structure for the program. Attempts to construct complicated programs in one giant leap resulted in code which was poorly structured and contained many *ad hoc* fixes. Such code proved very expensive, if not impossible, to maintain. Worse, because there had been no explicit statement of requirements, programs constructed in this way were often not what the intended user of the program wanted.

It was not long before engineers learnt to develop large systems in a series of stages, each of which produces a *baseline* which is the input to the next stages. This *stagewise* approach to software development is illustrated in Figure 2.1.

9

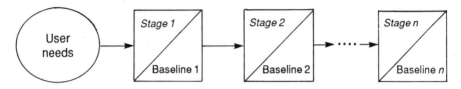

Figure 2.1   The stagewise model

A simple but popular example of the stagewise model has four stages:

- A *requirements analysis* stage, which produces a baseline that states what the system is required to do.

- A *design* stage, the baseline of which defines a structure for the system which will meet the requirements.

- An *implementation* stage, which implements the design to produce a working system.

- A *maintenance* stage, which produces a succession of working systems which perfect, adapt and correct the previous baseline.

The baseline produced by each stage forms the basis for the activities of the next stage. Each baseline before the system implementation is an abstract model of the system in which certain properties of the system are ignored. The earlier the baseline, the more abstract the model. Each stage may be viewed as the process of transforming an abstract model of the system into a less abstract one. Before it is approved a baseline is reviewed by verifying that it is consistent with previous baselines and by validating it against the user's needs.

The stagewise approach is a major improvement on the code and debug approach. It recognises the need to design the system before building it, as well as the need to confirm that the system under construction is what the user wants. Its most important deficiencies are that work on one stage cannot start before the previous stage is complete and that once a stage is complete the baseline it has produced cannot be changed. In practice system development just is not like this! The requirements for the system may change while the system is being designed; the implementation phase may reveal mistakes in the design of the system. The way to manage these problems is not to ignore a previous baseline which proves in some way to be inadequate, but to revise it. The *waterfall* model illustrated in Figure 2.2 recognises the feedback that occurs between the stages of the stagewise model and the need to change baselines produced by previous stages. The achievement of a baseline remains

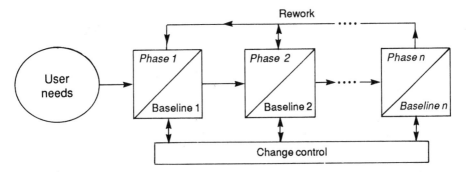

Figure 2.2   The generic waterfall model

a milestone which marks the start of a new and less abstract phase of the project. However, the model recognises that it may be necessary to revise baselines.

The waterfall model has been highly influential since it was first proposed by [Royce 70] in 1970. The names and content of the phases and baselines vary with such factors as the methodology used to develop the system, the quality standards which are in force and the culture—be it government, academic or commercial data processing. Most instantiations of the generic model include one or more phases which roughly correspond to each of the four stages of requirements analysis, design, implementation and maintenance.

For the waterfall model to be effective it is essential that changes to a baseline are rigorously controlled. A baseline is still the foundation for the subsequent phases of the lifecycle; it must not be altered without careful consideration of the consequences. The CM discipline of change control provides the framework for proposing a change, reviewing the proposal and then tracking the implementation of the change.

Figure 2.3 is an example of the way baselines may change in the course of a project. The first approved version of each baseline is shown as a solid box; subsequent versions of the baseline, which are shown as hollow boxes, are obtained by applying changes to the first version. The current version of a baseline at any moment is defined as the original version plus all approved changes which have been made to it.

Royce's description of the waterfall model recommends that only the most recently established baseline should be modified. It is not often possible to work so hygienically. In the example shown in Figure 2.3 the requirements specification is modified twice after the top level design has been approved. We live in the real world, with real users.

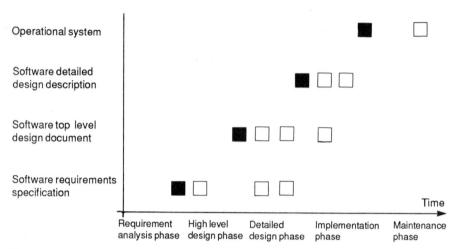

Figure 2.3   The evolution of baselines

2.2 BEYOND THE WATERFALL MODEL

Although the waterfall model is a widely used approach to developing software, its applicability to all kinds of software development is, to say the least, debatable. The major difficulty with the model is the emphasis it places upon producing complete and approved baselines before embarking upon the next phase of the lifecycle. Although the waterfall model allows baselines to be changed, the implication of the model is that such changes are highly undesirable. This approach works well when the requirements for the system are well understood, but it is much less effective if it is hard to capture requirements without some form of experimentation.

Consider a system which will be judged by the excellence of its user interface. The waterfall model invites the engineer to invest time and energy designing and then implementing a user interface only to discover, perhaps, that the needs of the user have been badly misunderstood. There are many other circumstances in which a phase cannot be properly completed without exploratory work in subsequent phases. Evolutionary development, prototyping and incremental development are three of the most popular alternatives to the waterfall model.

- *Evolutionary development.* With this approach a first-cut system is developed which is then modified until a system is obtained which meets the user's requirements. The approach is well suited to situations where users say, 'I can't tell you what I want but I'll know it when I see it'. It is also often used to develop highly innovative systems for which it is impossible to formulate a detailed statement of requirements and where correctness is difficult to assess. The danger with evolutionary development is that it is disturbingly similar to the code and debug model which was criticised at the beginning of this chapter.

- *Prototyping.* Prototyping requires the system to be built at least twice. All but the last implementation are prototypes, the purpose of which is to establish the detailed requirements of the system or to investigate the feasibility of an implementation strategy. Prototype implementations are allowed to make compromises on quality and functionality but must be discarded when they have served their purpose; this is the crucial difference between prototyping and evolutionary development.

- *Incremental development* Incremental development divides the system into parts which are produced in succession. Each increment of the system has its own lifecycle which may overlap in time with the lifecycles of other increments. This approach allows a part of the system to be completed quickly and to influence the development of subsequent increments.

These lifecycle models (or process models as they are increasingly called) are illustrated in Figure 2.4. Boehm's spiral model is a generalisation of all of these models. Each cycle of the spiral model produces a baseline and then plans the next cycle by evaluating the alternatives and their associated risks. The lifecycles illustrated in Figure 2.4 may be viewed as particular unwindings of the spiral model. See [Boehm 86] for further details.

Risk management is the key factor in the choice of lifecycle model. If it is too risky to develop the whole system at once, then incremental development should be considered. If the user interface requirements are uncertain then a prototype should be built. [Ould 90] describes in detail how to manage risk by selecting a suitable process model.

2.3 LIFECYCLE MODEL INDEPENDENT CM

There are two assumptions implicit in the waterfall model that make it inappropriate for at least some kinds of project. The first is the emphasis that it places on achieving a complete and approved baseline before starting the next phase of the lifecycle. The second is the assumption that an item is

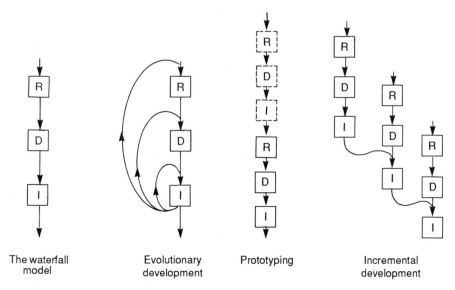

Figure 2.4   Lifecycle models for software development. R=Requirement, D=Design, I=Implementation

either a fully approved part of a baseline or it is not; the waterfall model does not provide for an item being granted limited approval such as provisional, experimental or prototype. For the purposes of CM, neither of these assumptions is desirable or necessary.

CM does not require that items which belong to different baselines are developed in any particular order. From the perspective of CM it is possible to develop an item without a complete specification; CM does not define what the approval criteria for the item should be. The question of when an item should be developed is an important one but is the concern of project rather than configuration management. To a large extent CM is concerned with managing the products of a project and is independent of the lifecycle process by which the products were constructed. Planning the project lifecycle is a vital aspect of project management, but it is beyond the scope of CM.

CM also needs to recognise that there is more to an item's status than whether or not it is part of an approved baseline. In practice an item has an associated *status* which corresponds to the level of approval it has achieved. An item which has achieved a high status in this sense will usually:

- *Have wide visibility.* A document with a status of draft may only be visible to a small group of reviewers; when it is promoted to approved status it will have much wider distribution. Software which has been tested and approved in isolation may have a status of unit tested, but must be tested in conjunction with the rest of the system to achieve the status of integration tested.

- *Be rigorously tested.* Software developed for a safety critical system might have three possible statuses: untested, tested and formally proven.

- *Be subject to strict change control.* A module which has been highly approved should not be changed without formal controls. Within an evolutionary development lifecycle, while the system is evolving it is changed frequently to match user requirements more closely; when these requirements are met the system becomes subject to strict change control and is only modified to fix faults.

- *Form the basis for subsequent work.* A design document which has been fully approved constitutes a stable basis for implementation.

The range of approval levels for an item depends on many factors including the lifecycle model and the type of item. In most cases a binary choice such as draft or baselined is inadequate.

By generalising from a rigid interpretation of the waterfall model, this book describes CM in a way which accommodates less restrictive models of software development, including those illustrated in Figure 2.4. However, although little mention is made of the waterfall model or of baselines, it is recognised that the waterfall model is by far the most commonly used model for software development; the treatment of CM which follows is entirely consistent with that model.

2.4 THE MAINTENANCE PHASE

The story of a software system does not end when its development is complete and it is delivered to its users. The system needs to be maintained, perhaps not by its developers, but by someone.

Software maintenance falls into three categories:

- *Corrective maintenance.* Changes to correct errors which were not discovered during the system's development.
- *Perfective maintenance.* Changes to the system required by its users which enhance the system without changing its basic functionality.
- *Adaptive maintenance.* Changes needed to accommodate changes in the environment in which the system operates.

Software maintenance is sometimes viewed as a poor relation of software development. It is not seen as a creative or highly skilled activity and is not the subject of much academic research. On the other hand, maintenance is rarely overlooked by industrial users of large software systems: the cost of maintaining a software system is, on average, between two and four times the cost of its initial development.

Although the discipline of CM is essential throughout the project lifecycle, it is never more important than during the maintenance phase. Software maintenance is concerned with changing existing software; CM provides precisely the framework that is needed to manage such changes. The problems listed in Section 1.1 can all arise during software maintenance. Indeed, these problems are often most acute during the maintenance phase when there are the largest number of software items to manage which exist in many versions and which are highly dependent upon each other. For this reason, many of the examples used in this book to illustrate aspects of CM will be drawn from the maintenance phase of a project.

Key Points

- Early models of the project lifecycle were either anarchic (like the code and debug model) or too restrictive (like the stagewise model).

- The waterfall model is a disciplined and practical model of the project lifecycle.

- A baseline produced by a phase of the waterfall model evolves subject to the CM discipline of change control.

- Modern models of the project lifecycle (evolutionary development, prototyping, incremental development and the spiral model) are more flexible than the waterfall model and address some of its deficiencies.

- The modern models, and maintenance phase of a project, demand a flexible approach to CM which is not based upon the waterfall model.

3

STRUCTURING SOFTWARE FOR CHANGE

Whatever view is taken of the project lifecycle, a software project must manage a wide variety of software items. In this book, the word *software* is very broadly interpreted to mean anything that can be stored on a magnetic medium such as a disc or tape. This broad interpretation is necessary and desirable. CM must be applied to source code, object code, executable programs, documentation, standards, tools, plans and test data—in short, to all the software which is important to the project.

This chapter classifies items into types and describes those relationships between items which are important for CM. It also discusses how software should be partitioned into items. The guiding principle is to structure the software so that it is easy to change. In a poorly structured system, to make a small functional change requires amendments to many items in various parts of the system. However good the CM procedures, the maintenance of such a system is fraught. By contrast, a change to a well structured system requires amendments to just a few items which are related to each other in a well defined way.

3.1 THE DESIGN ITEM HIERARCHY

In Chapter 1 an item was defined as software which may be treated as a unit for the purposes of CM. Sometimes it is useful to consider the entire system as a unit, for example when the complete system is to be issued to a client. At other times it is appropriate to consider a single procedure as a unit, for example when a programmer needs to amend just that one procedure independently of the rest of the system. The items of a system form a hierarchy in which a *composite* item consists of a set of *component* items. An item which, for CM purposes, is never decomposed into component items is called an *element*. Very often, but not always, an element is held as a single operating system file.

It is impossible to develop and maintain any but the simplest software system without dividing it into smaller, less complex and more manageable items. Decomposition of items is needed to achieve the four objectives listed below.

- *Manage complexity.* 'The technique of mastering complexity has been known since ancient times: *divide et impera* (divide and rule)' [Dijkstra 79]. Partitioning a complex system produces smaller and simpler components. Each of the components is easier to understand, design and manage than the whole.

- *Divide labour.* Responsibility for developing and maintaining parts of the system must be allocated to engineers. Near the top of the hierarchy, items are the responsibility of large teams which may belong to different organisations. Elements at the bottom of the hierarchy are typically developed by a single engineer over a period of a few weeks. To plan and manage a project, packages of work are decomposed in a work breakdown structure; there should be a close parallel between the item hierarchy and this work breakdown structure.

- *Produce a maintainable system.* Once software items have been developed they inevitably need to be changed: faults need to be corrected, new features are required and the environment in which the system operates changes. The item hierarchy should be such that a functional change to the system involves modifying items within one part of the hierarchy. If minor changes require modifications to diverse and distributed items of the hierarchy then the system will be hard to maintain.

- *Reuse items.* Where possible, items should be building blocks which can be used by many parts of the system. Hardware components are almost always reusable in this sense. The subroutine is the classic example of a reusable element of code; more general and powerful ways of structuring software for reuse will be discussed later in this chapter. It must also be possible to assemble different configurations of a system by combining items from the hierarchy in different ways.

Figure 3.1 shows part of the item hierarchy for a general purpose database management system (DBMS). The lowest level items in the hierarchy are the elements of the system. Composite items such as User Documentation and Query Processing are no more than the sum of their component elements.

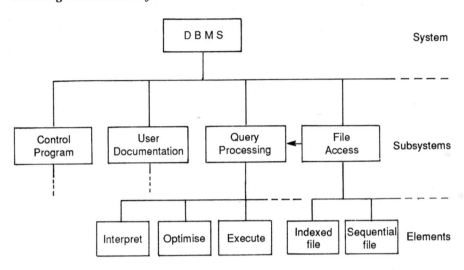

Figure 3.1   The item hierarchy for a database management system

Every element appears once and only once in the hierarchy. This does not mean that an element in one part of the hierarchy cannot make use of an element in another part. Elements in the Query Processing item of Figure 3.1 use elements of the File Access item; however, this relationship between items is quite different from the 'part-of' relationship which defines the hierarchy. The item hierarchy should not be confused with a module structure chart, as described, for example, in [Constantine 79], which shows how modules of the system make calls to other modules.

Not all items fit into this strict hierarchy. Many configuration items cut across the hierarchy, selecting and rejecting elements in order to achieve a particular purpose. For example, the DBMS might be configured to include the elements which are suitable for Unix rather than some other operating system platform, or to include those elements which are needed to run programs which use the DBMS but not those needed to develop new programs. These items are not shown in the hierarchy of Figure 3.1. The items that are part of the strict hierarchy are called *design items*; this name suggests their role as units of design which evolve as a single entity. A configuration item is not, in general, a design item.

How far should items be decomposed in the item hierarchy? To rephrase the question, how large should an element be? As a guideline, any software which can usefully be modified independently of other software should be an item. If items are insufficiently decomposed then:

• A small change requires a new version of a large item.

- Because an item should only be modified in one way at one time, the scope for parallel development is limited.

- It is not possible to select different combinations of elements to assemble different configurations which meet different requirements.

On the other hand, if items are too finely decomposed then the management of these items, in particular how they fit together, is unnecessarily complicated. Imagine trying to assemble a system by piecing together elements each of which contains only one line of code!

There is a plethora of specialised terminology which is used to describe items at different levels in the design hierarchy. For example, US standards refer to the top of the hierarchy as a Computer Software Configuration Item (CPCI), intermediate levels as Computer Software Components (CPCs) and the bottom level as Computer Software Units (CSUs). [IEEE-1042 87] gives examples of similar terms. Most CM tools also have their own terminology for items at different levels in the hierarchy. This book tries to keep its terminology simple: the item at the top of the design hierarchy is referred to as the system; the bottom level comprises elements; an item which is neither an element nor the entire system is sometimes called a subsystem.

3.2 SOURCE AND DERIVED ELEMENTS

A key distinction between elements is whether an element is derived by a program from other elements or whether it is constructed manually. An element which is constructed by automatic processing of other elements is called a derived element; an element which is not derived but is constructed manually is a called a source element. Important examples of derived elements include object modules, which are derived from source code using a compiler, and executable programs, which are derived from object modules using a linker. Figure 3.2 shows eight elements of a small system. The unshaded elements are source elements; the shaded elements are derived from the source elements using first a compiler and then a linker.

Derived elements should not be confused with binary elements, i.e. elements which contain bytes which do not represent text. A text element may be derived; for example, the C code produced by a C++ preprocessor is derived. Conversely a binary element is not necessarily derived; for example, a wordprocessor document usually includes control bytes which describe how the document should be formatted but is nevertheless a source element.

Sometimes it is not obvious whether an element is a source or derived element. Suppose a project has a standard format for source code which is defined by a program template. To write a new program, an engineer first

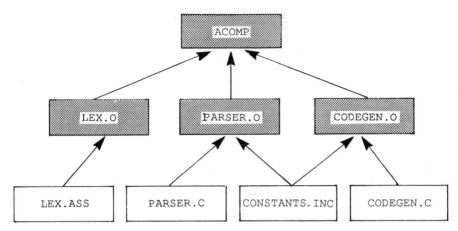

Figure 3.2   Source and derived elements of a small system

copies the template and then fills in the blank fields. This element is updated manually and should therefore be treated as a source element. Although it is constructed initially by copying the master template, it cannot be recreated by automatic processing.

In an ideal software engineering environment only source elements would need to be managed; derived elements would be constructed from source elements as and when required. If the three object modules in Figure 3.2 were deleted, for example to save disc space, they could be rederived from the source elements when the executable program ACOMP needed to be relinked. This is an attractively simple way of managing derived elements and is the basic approach of most CM tools. In fact, managing derived elements is not so simple. The rest of this section highlights complications which arise in practice, and outlines ways of dealing with them which will be described in more detail by subsequent chapters.

The source elements may not be available

In some circumstances the source elements used to construct a derived element may not be available. A software tool or a part of a large system may be provided by a third party who does not supply source code. In this case the derived element cannot be rederived and therefore should never be deleted.

The cost of derivation

It is not practical to rebuild a derived element every time it is needed: building the executable program of a large system may take hours of computer time. On the other hand, keeping all versions of all derived elements indefinitely may be very wasteful of disk space. A compromise is needed in which a derived element which is small, or frequently used, or expensive to rebuild is preserved while other derived items are deleted to release disk space.

The definition of the derivation procedure

How is ACOMP derived from its source elements? The answer is partly provided by Figure 3.2 which shows the elements from which each derived element is built. However, Figure 3.2 does not describe how CODEGEN.O is derived from CODEGEN.C; for example, it does not describe the options which should be passed to the C compiler. This vital information must not be left to chance but must be precisely defined by software which is itself managed as an item. The simplest approach is to give a procedural description of how derived elements are constructed. The description corresponding to Figure 3.2 might be the following:

```
ASSEMBLE LEX.ASS
CCOMPILE PARSER.C C
CCOMPILE CODEGEN.C
LINK PARSER.O, LEX.O, CODEGEN.O EXE=ACOMP
```

This constitutes a simple model of the system. It identifies the component elements of the system and describes how the derived elements are built. Such a description of the structure of a system is called a system model. The system model evolves as the structure of the system evolves. It is a CM principle that the system model must be explicit, unambiguous and managed as an item in its own right.

In the above example the entire system is described by one system model element. For a large system there may be many system model elements which describe the structure of parts of the system and how the parts fit together. The language used to model system structure varies greatly between different software engineering environments.

Source elements change

A derived element is constructed using a particular version of each source element. If a derived element is deleted and needs to be rebuilt, then the correct version of each source element must be used. This requires that:

●   The versions of the source elements needed to build the derived element are known.

- These versions are still available to build the derived element.

- There is an effective way for the build process to select these versions.

The tools used to build derived elements change

As well as being dependent upon source elements, a derived element also depends upon the state of the environment when it was derived. In an abstract sense, the derived elements shown in Figure 3.2 depend as much on the C compiler, the linker and the C library as upon the source elements shown in the figure. An upgrade to the C compiler may change the behaviour of an executable program. A frequently heard complaint after a new version of a compiler is installed is that source code which compiled cleanly with the old version of the compiler registers errors with the new, and more strict, version.

The way to tackle problems of this kind is to manage tools as items which are subject to the same controls as source code. The tools to be managed should include everything in the environment which affects how elements are derived, for example, compilers, linkers and the operating system platform. A new version of a tool should not be used before it has been thoroughly tested, nor should it be installed at a critical time in the project lifecycle, for example just before a major release, and it must be possible to revert to the previous version of the tool if something goes badly wrong. The requirements for managing source code which changes apply equally to tools which change.

Temporary modifications to derived elements

Derived elements should only be updated by amending the corresponding source elements and then rebuilding the derived element. Despite the protestations of CM purists, it is sometimes necessary to shortcut this procedure and to modify a derived element manually. For example, to correct a fault in a continuously running system it may be necessary to modify an executable program directly, perhaps because to rebuild and reinstall the program would require shutting the system down.

Manual changes to derived elements should only be made if there is no practical alternative. If a derived element must be modified manually then the modification should be viewed as temporary. The details of the change should be recorded and the derived element should be rederived from amended source elements as soon as possible. If the manual change to the derived element is intended to be permanent then the element is not really a derived element at all, and needs to be managed as a source element.

3.3 Dependencies between Items

Much of CM is concerned with controlling change: assessing the impact of a change before it is made, identifying and managing the multiple versions of items which a change generates, rebuilding derived elements after source elements are changed and keeping track of all the changes that are made to a system. Change is hard to manage because items depend upon each other. An apparently minor change to one element may propagate to items which depend upon it, directly or indirectly, so that consequential changes are needed throughout the system.

Formally, an item X is *dependent* upon an item Y if a change to Y might require changes to X for X to remain correct; if X requires a compatible version of Y for X to fulfil its purpose then X is dependent upon Y. If X is not dependent upon Y, then Y can be arbitrarily changed without affecting the correctness of X. Dependencies arise between many different type of items:

- The implementation of an item is dependent upon its specification. A change to the specification will probably require the implementation to change. The specification does not depend upon its implementation because the correctness of the specification is assessed independently of its implementation.

- A derived element is dependent upon its source elements in the strongest possible sense. A change to a source element requires new versions of the elements which are derived from it. By definition, a derived element cannot be changed directly. The dependency of a derived element upon the elements from which it is built is called a *build dependency*.

- Whenever an element of code calls another, the calling element is dependent upon the called element. If the `Execute` element shown in Figure 3.1 calls the `Indexed_file` element to access a database file then the `Indexed_file` element cannot be changed without regard to the needs of the `Execute` element. The `Execute` element is therefore dependent upon the `Indexed_file` element, but not vice versa.

- The user documentation of a system and the code of the system are dependent upon each other. These two items are maintained in parallel; neither can be assessed or changed independently of the other.

In this book many diagrams show dependencies between items. In all cases, a dependency of X upon Y is indicated by an arrow from Y to X (Figure 3.3). Reading along the direction of the arrow should be read as 'affects'. The arrow indicates the direction in which change propagates. See, for example, the lifecycle models illustrated in Chapter 2, the system model

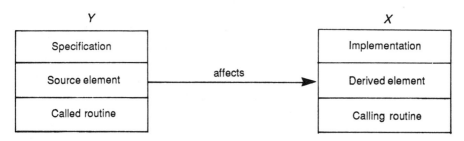

Figure 3.3   X depends on Y

of Figure 3.2 and the arrow from the File Access subsystem to the Query Processing subsystem which calls it in Figure 3.1.

Dependency is the fundamental relationship between items which CM must control. If all items were independent of each other, most if not all of the problems of CM would vanish. Structuring items to minimise dependencies is therefore an important objective in designing the item hierarchy.

3.4 DESIGNING THE ITEM HIERARCHY

Determining the item hierarchy for a system amounts to no more nor less than designing the system. Design by top-down functional decomposition starts with the item at the top of the hierarchy, i.e. the entire system, and iteratively divides items into components which perform different functions. More modern approaches like object oriented design propose that items in the hierarchy should correspond to objects in the system's environment and that it is sometimes best to design the system from the bottom up; see [Booch 91] for details. In Figure 3.1 the decomposition of the Query Processing subsystem has a functional feel to it, whereas the structure of the File Access subsystem is more object oriented.

Whatever method is used to design the item hierarchy, it is important that the dependencies between items are minimised. Where items depend on each other then they should, as far as possible, be located in the same part of the design hierarchy. Note how minimising dependencies between items achieves the four objectives for item decomposition listed in Section 3.1.

The classical software engineering criteria of coupling and cohesion may be used to evaluate an item hierarchy. [Constantine 79] defines coupling and cohesion for elements of procedural code, however, the concepts generalise to all types of item. Each item within the hierarchy should be cohesive: it should possess a single defining characteristic that relates its components. The coupling between items in different parts of the hierarchy should be weak; in CM terms, this means that dependencies should be minimised.

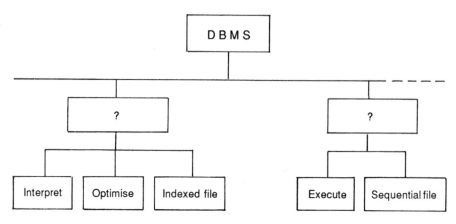

Figure 3.4   A poorly structured item hierarchy

Coupling and cohesion are two sides of the same coin. Swapping the Indexed_file and the Execute elements, as shown in Figure 3.4, gives an item hierarchy in which the two subsystems are tightly coupled but in which neither subsystem is cohesive. Note that it is no longer possible to give a succinct and descriptive name to either of the subsystems—a sure sign that they are not cohesive.

By no means all of the software for a database management system is shown in Figure 3.1. For example, each subsystem has its own test programs and test data; these elements are natural components of the corresponding subsystem.

Derived elements also need a home in the design item hierarchy. A derived element which is built from source elements which all belong to the same subsystem is a natural component of that subsystem. On the other hand, the executable program for the database management system is derived from source elements which are part of many subsystems. Where should this derived element be placed in the hierarchy? To answer this question, one of the source elements from which an element is derived is designated as the *primary source*; the derived element is then part of the same subsystem as its primary source. The primary source is usually selected so that other source elements do not depend on it. For the database management system of Figure 3.1 the Control Program subsystem, which contains the highest level modules in the calling hierarchy and controls the rest of the system, will contain the primary source of the executable program.

Minimising dependencies between items is the most important consideration when designing an item hierarchy, but it is not the only one. As an example, consider a system which must be highly secure against unauthorised use. The code which ensures the security of such a system is usually isolated in one subsystem, often called the 'security kernel', even though many other parts of the system depend upon this subsystem. There are several benefits to this approach: the subsystem can be developed to more stringent quality criteria, formal methods can be used to develop the subsystem and it can be developed by a team with expertise in computer security. Often these kinds of considerations coincide with the objective of minimising dependencies between items; when they conflict, a balance needs to be struck.

3.5 INFORMATION HIDING

The `Execute` element of Figure 3.1 calls the `Indexed_file` element. It is therefore dependent upon it: the `Indexed_file` element cannot be changed without regard to the way it is used by the `Execute` element. The `Execute` element does not, however, depend on all parts of the `Indexed_file` element. For example, the details of the algorithms used by the `Indexed_file` element can be changed without affecting the `Execute` element, or any other item in the hierarchy.

Information hiding is a technique, first described in detail by [Parnas 72], for restricting the way in which one item depends upon another. The principle of information hiding is that an item has two parts:

- The *interface* is the only part of the item which is visible to other items. It specifies precisely the characteristics of the item which other items need to know; it scrupulously avoids describing details of the item which need not concern other items. The interface is also called the specification or public part of an item.

- The *body* of the item is not visible to any other item. All decisions about how the requirements of the interface are implemented are hidden in the body. The body of an item can be changed freely providing it remains consistent with the interface. The body of an item is also called its implementation or private part.

Information hiding can be used to hide both algorithms and data structures in the body of an item as shown by the following two examples.

- *A sort procedure.* The interface of a procedure to sort an array of integers describes how an unsorted array is passed to the procedure and how the sorted array is returned. The algorithm used to sort the integers is hidden in the body of the procedure.

- *A dictionary item .* The following code is the interface of an Ada package which maintains a dictionary of words and their meanings. The word and its meaning are both character strings and the type `STRING_ARRAY` is an array of strings.

```
package DICTIONARY is
      procedure Add_meaning (word, meaning: STRING);
      procedure Delete_meaning (word, meaning: STRING);
      function Get_meanings (word: STRING) return
         STRING_ARRAY;
end DICTIONARY;
```

The body of the Ada package hides the data structures used to store the dictionary: words may be stored in a list, a hash table or a B-tree; the meaning of a word may be stored with the word or there may be pointer from the word to its meaning; the dictionary may be stored in memory or on disc. All of these decisions are hidden within the body of the Ada package. Any implementation decision which affects users of the Dictionary package, for example any bound on the number of meanings for a word, should be described in the interface.

Dividing an item into an interface and a body allows all dependencies on the item to be restricted to dependencies on its interface, as shown in Figure 3.5. Usually the interface of an item is much smaller than its body and many changes can be confined to the body of the item. A change to the body of an item is guaranteed not to affect other items, providing the body remains consistent with the interface.

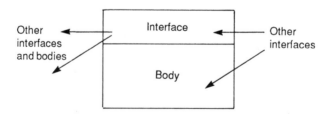

Figure 3.5   Restricting dependencies to the interface

Should the interface and body be distinct items that may evolve separately? In less abstract terms, should the interface and body of an element be held in separate files? The answer to this question varies with the size and complexity of the interface. The interface to a large subsystem is usually a separate item; the interface is part of the subsystem, but it is a particularly significant part which must be carefully managed. It will not change as often as the elements which form the body of the subsystem, but when it does the change affects other subsystems. On the other hand, the interface to the procedure which sorts an array of integers is very small; it probably is not worth while to manage the interface to this item as a distinct element with its own version history and its own relationships with other elements.

3.6 THE HIERARCHY OF INTERFACES

The two examples of item interfaces and bodies given in the previous section were for elements. Composite items in the design item hierarchy also have interfaces. A composite item is the aggregation of all its component items; the interface of a composite item is a subset of the aggregation of the interfaces of its components.

As an example of a composite item consider a subsystem which draws line graphics on a raster display. This subsystem consists of four elements which:

- Clear the screen.

- Draw a line on the screen.

- Convert a line from user to screen coordinates.

- Rasterise a line, i.e. convert a line to pixels.

Each of these elements has a single procedure call as its interface. The interface of the graphics subsystem includes only those element interfaces that should be visible to other subsystems. The interfaces of the first two elements fall into this category; the purpose of the subsystem is to provide precisely these services. On the other hand, the third and fourth elements should only be visible within the graphics subsystem.

Once interfaces have been defined for all items at all levels in the hierarchy, then the visibility of these interfaces from different parts of the hierarchy is defined by the following rule:

An item X may depend upon another item Y, via the interface of Y, only if X is a component of the parent of Y.

The effect of this rule is illustrated in Figure 3.6. The element labelled X cannot depend on the interface of the `Rasterise_line` element because X is not a component of the Graphics subsystem. On the other hand, X may depend upon the interface of the Graphics subsystem, and therefore on the `Draw_line` and `Clear_screen` elements, because X is a component of the parent of the Graphics subsystem. `Draw_line` can depend upon the interfaces of all the other elements of the Graphics subsystem. The rule for

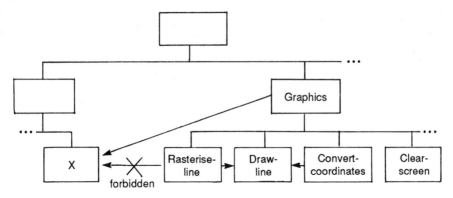

Figure 3.6   Item hierarchy showing permitted and forbidden dependencies

visibility of interfaces is analogous to the scoping rules for variables in a block structured programming language.

Information hiding at each level in the item hierarchy, together with the rule limiting item visibility, is a powerful technique for managing change and containing its effects. A change to an item can be classified by the extent to which other items might be affected by the change. For example, a change to the graphics subsystem falls into one of three categories:

- A change which is confined to the bodies of the component elements of the subsystem.

- A change to an interface of an element, but not an interface which is included in the interface of the Graphics subsystem.

- A change to an interface of an element which is part of the interface of the Graphics subsystem, for example the interface to Draw_line.

The more items that might be affected by a change, the more carefully the change must be reviewed. A change to the interface of Draw_line needs to be agreed by all users of the Graphics subsystem; a change to the interface of Rasterise_line can be agreed within the team responsible for the Graphics subsystem; a change to the body of Draw_line which does not affect its interface is independent of all other elements of the system.

3.7 DESCRIBING THE INTERFACE

The item interface should provide a complete and precise description of those aspects of the item upon which other items may depend. In practice, interfaces are rarely either complete or precise. The description of the interface to the Dictionary package in Section 3.5 is far from complete. It does not describe the order in which meanings are returned by the Get_meaning function; nor does it indicate how the package responds to unusual or error conditions. For example, what happens if an attempt is made to delete a meaning for a word which is not in the dictionary? Furthermore, it is left to the reader's intuition to realise that the meanings for a word returned by Get_meaning are precisely those which have been supplied by Add_meaning but not removed by Delete_meaning.

One way in which a project can improve the quality of interface documentation is to use a standard structure, defined by a template, to describe interfaces. Templates guarantee that the basic properties of an interface are described in a uniform way. The fields of an interface template vary with the programming language used and the nature of the system. A typical template for code written in a procedural language includes the following fields:

- *Name.* The name of the procedure.

- *Purpose.* A prose description of the purpose of the procedure.

- *Input parameters.* The type and meaning of data passed to the procedure.

- *Output parameters.* The type and meaning of data returned by the procedure and its relationship to the input parameters.

- *Side effects.* The properties of the procedure not implied by a description of its inputs and outputs; for example, the effect of the procedure upon subsequent calls to this and related procedures.

- *Errors and exceptions.* The conditions which preclude the normal execution of the procedure, and the effect of these conditions.

- *Constraints.* The assumptions made by the procedure and the constraints, such as timing, to which it conforms.

There are two pitfalls to avoid when describing the interface of an item. The first is that natural languages such as English are notoriously ambiguous. Formal specification languages are the only sure way to describe an interface unambiguously. See [Cohen 86] for an introduction to formal specification languages.

The second pitfall is that, in striving to be complete and precise, the interface may fall into the trap of describing the implementation of the item. There are several approaches to this problem. One is to describe the effect of a procedure in terms of subsequent calls to the same and related procedures. For example, the effect of the Delete_meaning procedure is that a subsequent call to `Get_meaning` does not return the meaning that has been deleted. Another approach is to describe related procedures in terms of their effect upon an abstract model of the data which the procedures maintain. Using this approach, the Dictionary package would be described in terms of a data structure containing words and meanings. Note that the abstract model serves only to specify the item; the body of the item may use an entirely different data structure to implement the specification.

Although it is not usually necessary to give a complete and mathematically precise description of all item interfaces, considerable care should be devoted to clarifying the important interfaces of the system.

3.8 THE INTERFACE AS A CONTRACT

An item interface may be regarded as a contract which the defines the conditions which the body of the item must fulfil. An interface, like any contract, must be precise, complete, enforced, agreed, visible and only changed subject to careful controls.

Enforcing an interface means ensuring that the body of the item does indeed implement the interface and that other items use the interface accurately. For items of code, software tools can go some way towards enforcing an interface. For example, many compilers check that a procedure is called with the correct number and type of arguments. The Ada program library makes these checks possible even if the elements of code are compiled separately; see Chapter 8 for further details. In general, however, an interface is enforced by quality control activities such as testing and reviews.

An interface must be explicitly agreed by everyone with a legitimate interest in it, including the engineers who develop and maintain the body of the item as well as all users of the interface. Once agreed, the interface must be stored securely and visibly. Like all software, interfaces need to be revised. Changes must be negotiated and agreed by everyone who depends upon the interface, including all the signatories to the version which is to be superseded. The transition to a new version of an interface must be carefully managed to ensure that different parts of the system are not using incompatible versions. CM methods and tools for achieving these objectives are the subject of the rest of this book.

The history of software development is rich with projects which have come to grief when the component items of the system are integrated. The cause of this grief is usually that the interfaces between the subsystems have not been defined and controlled with sufficient care. Sorting out poorly defined interfaces during the integration phase of a project is both costly and frustrating—but it is also avoidable.

Key Points

- A software system is structured as items which are subject to CM.

- Design items form a strict hierarchy in which a composite item comprises a set of component items. Indecomposable items are called elements.

- Elements are either source elements or derived elements; different CM techniques are needed to manage these two types of element.

- Dependencies between items is the main source of the complexity which CM must manage. The design item hierarchy must therefore be structured to minimise dependencies.

- The principle of information hiding restricts dependencies on an item to dependencies on its interface. Both composite items and elements have interfaces.

- The interface is a contract which describes the services provided by an item to its clients. Interfaces must be defined and controlled with particular care.

4

VERSION MANAGEMENT

During the development of an item it evolves until it first reaches a state where it fulfils its purpose. The story does not end there: mistakes not found during the item's development need to be corrected, the item may need to be adapted to match changes in its environment and the item may need to be enhanced. Each of these changes produces a new *revision* of the item. An item may also need to meet similar but different requirements at the same time; a *variant* of the item is needed for each of these requirements. For example, there might be two variants of a subroutine which returns the calendar date: one suitable for Unix and the other for OS/2.

An instance of an item, each of its variants and revisions, is called an item *version*. Depending on the context, the unqualified word item means either all versions of the item or one particular version. This chapter describes how versions arise, and what methods and tools are available for managing them.

4.1 CONTROLLED ITEMS

While an item is being developed it is frequently changed and evolves through a succession of temporary and incorrect states. These transient states of the item are visible only to its developer. At some stage in its development the item reaches a stable form which is worth preserving. Typically this is when the item is first made available to engineers other than its developer, for example for testing or review. At this stage the item is placed under CM control.

The immediate consequence of CM control is that the item is frozen. Before it was frozen, the working version of the item was mutable: it could be modified without creating a new version. Once frozen, the item can only be changed by creating a new version. Other aspects of CM control are that the item is reliably stored and is identified in a way which distinguishes it from all other versions of the item.

Very often, an item is promoted through several stages of approval. For example, an element of code is first tested in isolation from other elements (unit tested), then tested in conjunction with other elements (integration tested) and then formally audited prior to release. Traditional CM defines rigorous and rigid procedures for controlling items which are highly approved. This sort of CM is an adjunct to project management; it controls and records changes to approved baselines, audits software releases for consistency with the planned content of the release and provides a basis for quality control activities.

More modern approaches to CM enlarge the scope of traditional CM to include support for programmers as well as managers. They emphasise the importance of controlling the way in which derived items are built, of storing versions of items efficiently and reliably, and of allowing many engineers to work together in a productive way. This book assumes that items are controlled from an early stage in their evolution, at the latest from the time when they are of concern to more than one person. The challenge, of course, is to match the level of CM control to the context.

4.2 REVISIONS

Controlled items need to be changed for many reasons. Chapter 2 noted that a fully approved baseline may need to be revised during later phases of the project lifecycle. Controlled items which have not been fully approved are subject to more frequent change, for example, a unit tested element of code may require many revisions during integration testing before it is fully approved. During the maintenance phase of a project, revisions are needed to correct, perfect and adapt the software.

The CM procedure for changing a controlled, and therefore frozen, item is to create a new revision of the item. Every item exists as a time ordered sequence of revisions. Each revision, except the first, has a predecessor and each, except the most recent, has a successor. Collectively the revisions of an item represent its history. In practice, a revision of an item is usually created by taking a copy of the most recent revision which is then modified to produce the new revision.

Figure 4.1 shows a succession of revisions of an item. It illustrates the CM principle that old revisions should not be overwritten. There are several reasons for preserving old revisions of an item:

- Old revisions may be part of a system which is in operational use; an operational fault should be investigated using precisely those items which are used in the operational system.

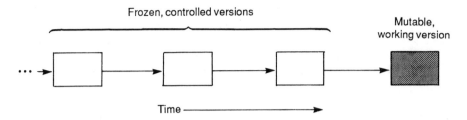

Figure 4.1   Successive revisions of an item

- It is possible to revert to the unrevised item if the revision has unexpected and undesirable side effects.

- Users of the item may continue to use the unrevised item if they wish. For example, a programmer may wish to work with stable versions of library items.

The model for revising an item which forms the basis of most CM tools is illustrated in Figure 4.2. All controlled items are held in a *library* which is managed by a CM tool. When an item needs to be revised, a revision of the item is checked out of the library. This operation creates a copy of the item in the developer's private workspace. This copy is outside the scope of the CM tool and may be freely changed by the developer. When the change to the item is complete, the revised item is checked into the library, thereby creating a new controlled revision of the item. The previous revision of the item is not overwritten but is preserved in the library.

Except where describing specific tools, this book uses the terms *check out* and *check in* for the two basic operations on the software library. Some other authors and tools use different words. For example, many tools use the words reserve and replace; unfortunately replace suggests, quite wrongly, that the previous revision is overwritten.

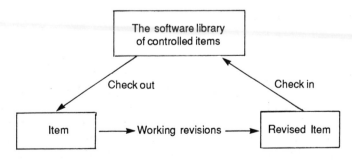

Figure 4.2   The principle of the software library

In the developer's private workspace an item evolves through many temporary and inconsistent states before it is checked into the library. For example, a text element being modified by a screen editor is changed by almost every keystroke! These modifications are beyond the control of CM. Nevertheless, experienced engineers create working revisions of the item as snapshots of its evolution. Working revisions serve as backups which prevent intermediate results from being jeopardised by further experimental work or by machine failure. Formally, working revisions are not subject to CM: they need not be identified, no other part of the system depends on them and they are normally deleted when the item is checked into the library. Different software tools and environments create and store working revisions in different ways. For example, editors running under the VMS operating system create a working revision whenever the editor writes the element to disk; VMS stores each working revision as a file version; old file versions are cleared out by the VMS PURGE command.

4.3 VARIANTS

As well as evolving over time, some items need to meet different but related requirements at the same time. A variant of an item represents the need for one item to meet conflicting requirements at the same time. For example, a program which is to run on several operating systems will have one variant of the item which manages disk files for each target operating system.

Variance, like revision, is a relationship between items. Unlike revision, one variant of an item is in no sense an improvement on another variant. The relationship of variance is symmetric: if *A* is a variant of *B* then *B* is a variant of *A*. A variant of an item will itself evolve and will therefore exist as a series of revisions. A specific instance of an item is identified by which variant of the item it is, and which revision of that variant. The set of all items that are variants or revisions of each other constitute all the versions of the item.

4.3.1 Temporary variants

Variants of items are either temporary or permanent. A *temporary variant* is one that will later be merged with other variants of the item. Figure 4.3 illustrates a classic problem of version management. Versions 1, 2, 3, 4, 5 and 6 are revisions in the main line of descent for the item. When version 3 of the item is under development a fault is discovered in version 2 of the item which is in use at a customer site. A solution to the problem is needed urgently and cannot wait until version 3 of the item is approved. To accommodate the fix to the problem a variant of the item is created and identified as FIX.1. This variant is then supplied to the customer.

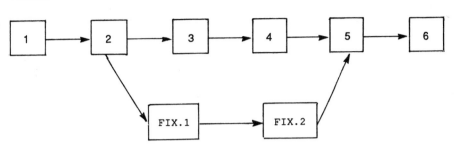

Figure 4.3   A branch line of descent for temporary variants

There are now two versions of the item: version FIX.1, which contains the urgent fix to version 2, and version 3, which contains all the planned improvements to version 2—but not the urgent fix. Neither of the versions can be said to be strictly better than the other. Once version 3 is approved, a change may need to be made to both version 3 and version FIX.1, thereby creating versions 4 and FIX.2. This uncomfortable and risky situation is sometimes known as double maintenance or double baselining. The solution is to merge the branch line of descent which contains FIX.1 and FIX.2 with the main line as soon as possible. Version 5, which is obtained by merging versions 4 and FIX.2, then forms the unique basis for subsequent revisions.

Situations like this are quite common during software development and maintenance. If two engineers need to revise the same item at the same time, each creates a variant of the item; these two variants are later merged. Variants may also be used to explore alternative ways of designing or implementing an item; in this case merging the variants amounts to selecting the preferred variant and discarding the others.

The longer the lifetime of a temporary variant, the further it will diverge from versions in the main line of descent and the more difficult the task of merging the variants becomes. Temporary variants should be avoided whenever possible; when they are unavoidable they should be merged as soon as possible.

4.3.2 Permanent variants

Few software systems are for the use of a single client in a single environment. Most systems have many users who have different requirements and who require the system to operate in different environments. Imagine a software supplier providing a payroll system for the use of employers throughout the world. To maximise its potential market, variants of the payroll system are needed which match the varying needs and resources of different employers. Variants of this kind are permanent: they are not intended to be merged together. *Permanent variants* fall into three categories:

- *Varying user requirements.* Variants of the system are needed to match the different requirements of different users. This sort of variation is sometimes called customisation. If the payroll system is to be used in different countries then the system must communicate with its users in different national languages. The system must also vary to comply with the different employee and tax legislation of different countries. Large employers may require the payroll system to be customised for their particular needs, perhaps to produce a particular management report.

- *Varying platform*   The system must be implemented to use the resources provided by the platform on which it runs. Variations of the platform must be matched by corresponding variations of the system. To maximise its market, the payroll system must run on several operating systems. Different operating systems provide a similar service in different ways. For example, the way in which Unix and OS/2 return the calendar date is quite different, so there must be a variant for each operating system of an item in the payroll system which determines the calendar date.

  The system must cater for revisions as well as variations of its platform. Different revisions of OS/2 may require different variants of the payroll system. Note that these differences cannot, in general, be managed as revisions to the payroll system because they may be needed at the same time. The payroll system must exist simultaneously as variants which match the different revisions of OS/2. The variants are needed to supply clients who may or may not be using the latest revision of OS/2.

- *Variants for testing and debugging.* Items often exist as variants to meet particular requirements of the engineers developing or maintaining the system. For example, elements of code may contain assertions which check the integrity of internal data structures. Assertion checks are an effective way of detecting a fault sooner rather than later and can be an invaluable aid to software testing and debugging. Assertion checks are redundant to the function of the code and are not usually included in the released system, where the checks would be a waste of time and space. It may also be useful for testing and debugging to have available variants of the system which trace the flow of control through the code and print the value of variables at critical stages.

  Note that variants for testing and debugging are not temporary. Assertion checks should not be irreversibly removed but should be retained in a variant of the system throughout its life.

Managing variance is one of the hardest problems of CM. For a single system like the payroll system variance can arise in many dimensions: national language, tax and employee legislation, operating system platform, variants for debugging and temporary variants. The number of possible combinations in these dimensions can be alarmingly large, even for quite small systems. Usually the dimensions of variation are not completely independent. For example, the variant of the payroll system for French tax and employee legislation will always also use the French language. These kinds of constraints reduce the number of variants of the system that are actually needed, however, managing the constraints is itself a challenge for CM. How should CM ensure that a variant of the payroll system is not built which both complies with French legislation and communicates with its users in German?

4.4 METHODS AND TOOLS FOR MANAGING VARIANCE

One of the problems of variance is that it is often unplanned. Temporary variants are inherently unplanned, but permanent variants also have an unpleasant habit of popping up unexpectedly. For example, the payroll system described in the previous section was designed to run on Unix and to assume US legislation; only after the product proved successful in the United States did the marketing department demand that the system should run on other operating systems and be customised for employers in Europe.

Several approaches to managing variance are described in this section; each has its strengths and weaknesses. No single approach is adequate for all types of variance but between them they provide a way of dealing with variance when it arises and of structuring software so that the development of variant items can be managed.

4.4.1 Localising variance

Consider the problem of developing variants of the payroll system to run on several operating systems. The crudest solution is to maintain variants of all items which use the services of the operating system directly. The trouble with this approach is that it requires variants for items which make only incidental use of operating system services.

Consider an element of code which produces a complex report of employee salaries and depends upon the operating system solely to obtain the date and time to include on the frontsheet of the report. Most changes to this element will have nothing to do with the way the code obtains the date and time from the operating system; however, these changes must be made to every operating system variant of the element. Only changes to the way the code obtains the date and time will be specific to just one of the variants. This is another example of the double maintenance problem mentioned earlier, the situation here is even worse because it is permanent. Double maintenance contradicts a basic rule of structuring data: keep one fact in one place.

   The most effective technique for managing variance is to confine the differences between variants of the system to as few items as possible. Only these few items exist as a set of variants; other items are the same for all variants of the system. The variant items serve as interchangeable building blocks: a particular variant of the system is assembled by selecting one variant of each item. To avoid the double maintenance problem, variant items should contain as little as possible that is common to all the variants. In short, variance should be localised and variant items should contain nothing but variance.

   Localising variance for the payroll system can be achieved by isolating in one subsystem everything which depends upon the operating system platform. The body of this subsystem contains everything which varies for different operating systems. The interface to the subsystem is the same for all operating systems, so that the rest of the payroll system is independent of the operating system platform. The interface to one element of this subsystem is shown below and forms a part of the interface of the subsystem:

```
package CLOCK
   function get_date () return DATE;
   function get_time () return TIME;
   type DATE is
     record
       YEAR: INTEGER range 1980..2100;
       MONTH: INTEGER range 1..12;
       DAY: INTEGER range 1..31;
     end record;
   type TIME is
     record
       HOUR: INTEGER range 0..23;
       MINUTE: INTEGER range 0..59;
       SECOND: INTEGER range 0..59;
     end record;
end
```

   The package uses the system clock to determine the current date and time. There are variants of this element for each operating system. Although the interface is the same for all variants, the way the body of the element accesses the system clock varies for different operating system platforms.

   Structuring the payroll system in this way localises the variance caused by different operating system platforms within one subsystem. Providing the interface is not changed, the Unix variant of this subsystem can be changed independently of other variants and independently of the rest of the system.

   The objective of localising variance is to minimise the extent to which similar code is duplicated between several elements. Unfortunately it is often far from obvious how best to achieve this. For example, perhaps the type DATE defined by the CLOCK package should be an array of two integers: the year and the ordinality of the day in the year. Operating system independent code would then calculate the month and the day in the month. Whether or not this interface is an improvement upon the CLOCK package shown above depends upon how each operating system platform provides today's date.

Structuring software to localise variance is a hard problem which is made even harder if it is not known in advance what variants will be required. Determining the date and time using different operating system platforms is just a small example of the problem. The payroll system also needs an operating system independent interface to access disk files. A common interface for, say, Unix and OS/2 needs very careful design. This interface may be quite inappropriate if the payroll system ever needs to run on the VMS operating system.

All items which are variants of each other may be regarded as the same at some level of abstraction. Variants have significant similarities and significant differences; at some level of abstraction only the similarities matter. Sometimes, particularly for permanent variants for different platforms, the appropriate level of abstraction is that variant items should have the same interface. At other times the abstraction is less precisely defined and harder to model. If English and French language variants of the payroll system are needed, then all dialogue text must be maintained in both these national languages. The objective is then to structure the system so that all text visible to the user of the payroll system is localised in national language dependent items. These items should not contain anything which is independent of the national language, for example the way the text is displayed. The abstraction which relates variants of these items is that the text each contains should have the same meaning, although the language used to express the meaning varies.

4.4.2 Merging variants

By their nature, temporary variants are eventually merged. Sometimes merging amounts to no more than discarding one of the variants, for example an experimental variant which has proved a failure. More usually, merging variants involves combining the improvements which have been made in each of the variant lines of descent. In the example of Figure 4.3 versions 4 and FIX.2 both contain improvements on version 2 which need to be combined to produce version 5.

Many CM tools, including DSEE, RCS and CMS, at least partially automate the merging of variant elements. All these tools use essentially the same algorithm. A three-way comparison is made between the latest revision of the two variants to be merged and the latest revision of their common ancestor, called the *base version*. In Figure 4.3 version 2 is the base version for versions 4 and FIX.2. The merged version is constructed by scanning these three versions in parallel. If the two variants are the same then the merged version contains that text. If the two variants differ but one is the same as the base version, then the variant which is different from the base version is included in the merged version. If all three versions are different then there is a conflict which the tool does not resolve. RCS and CMS flag conflicts in the merged version which must then be resolved manually. The merge operation in DSEE is interactive: the user is asked to select an alternative whenever a conflict arises and is offered the option of resolving the conflict manually.

A merge tool can also be used to apply the same revision to several elements, for example to permanent variants. Suppose X and Y are variants which must be revised in the same way. The revision is first applied manually to X to produce X'. The revision is then applied to Y by merging X' and Y using X as the base version. This approach is better than revising both X and Y manually, but it only works well when X and Y are very similar. Even then the techniques described in the next two subsections are a more reliable way of managing similar permanent variants.

The limitation of most tools that merge variants is that they do not understand the meaning of the texts to be merged. The tool must determine when two fragments of text match. This begs the question of how large a fragment should be (one line, several lines,...?). An intelligent tool would use the meaning of the text to determine the fragments to compare. In practice, merge tools often make incorrect assessments of how variants should be merged or, at best, register conflicts which, with a little knowledge of the meaning of the text, could be resolved automatically; see [Reps 88] for examples.

A merge tool is a very useful component of a software engineering environment, but it should not be trusted blindly. Even if the tool registers no conflicts, the result of the merge operation should be carefully reviewed.

4.4.3 Storing variants within one source element

Localising variance as recommended in Section 4.4.1 is not always possible. A debug variant of procedural code might contain trace statements or assertion checks; to fulfil their purpose these debug statements should be distributed throughout the code and not be localised in one part of the system. Alternatively a new client might require the system to be customised in a way which its designers did not not foresee and which requires changes to items throughout the hierarchy.

One technique for managing variance which cannot be localised is to represent all the variants within a single source element and derive different variants by processing the element in different ways. Conditional compilation in FORTRAN is a simple and early example of this approach. Depending upon the options chosen when the FORTRAN compiler is invoked, lines of source code with an *X* in column one are either ignored or compiled. In this way an element of FORTRAN source embodies two variants.

The C programming language takes this principle a stage further. The C compiler incorporates a preprocessor which performs macro substitution, conditional compilation and inclusion of named files. Lines in C source text which start with a # are directives to the preprocessor. A preprocessor directive of the form

```
#define macro-name macro-value
```

assigns a string of characters to a macro. Macros may also be assigned a value by the command which invokes the C compiler. If the preprocessor subsequently encounters the name of the macro it substitutes its value for its name. [Kernighan 78] gives details of the algorithm used for macro substitution and also describes how to define and use macros with arguments. Preprocessor directives to control conditional compilation take the form

```
#if constant-expression
... C code ...
#else
... C code ...
#endif
```

The constant-expression, which will include macros in its terms, evaluates to either zero (false) or non-zero (true). If it is true then lines between the #else and #endif are ignored; if it is false then lines between the test and the #else (or, in the absence of an #else, the #endif) are ignored.

A C function which sorts an array into ascending order is shown below:

```
bubble(v,n)     /* sort v[0] ... v [n-1]
                   into ascending order */
TYPE v[];       /* TYPE is either int, char, float
                   or double */
int n;
{
int i, swop, temp;
#if DEBUG
     if ( n < 1 )
     printf ("bubble called with invalid argument\n");
#endif
```

```
     do {
        swop = 0;
        for ( i = 0; i<n-1; i++ )
           if ( v[i] > v [i+1] ) {
              temp = v[i];
              v[i] = v[i+1];
              v[i+1] = temp;
              swop = 1;
           }
     } while ( swop == 0 );
#if DEBUG
     for (i = 0; i<n-1; i++)
           if ( v[i] > v [i+1] )
           printf ("Failure within bubble\n");
#endif
     }
```

The C preprocessor generates variants of the function from this one source
element in two dimensions. Firstly, depending upon the value of the macro
DEBUG, the function will check that the length of the array passed to the
function is at least 1 and will check that, at the end of the function, the array
is indeed in ascending order. Secondly, the macro TYPE defines the type of
array which the function sorts.

A specific variant is selected by compiling the function in a context where
the macros TYPE and DEBUG have been given appropriate values; for
example,

```
#define DEBUG 0          /* i.e. false */
#define TYPE int
```

These two define directives may be part of the same source element which
contains the rest of the function. Alternatively, the define directives may be
in a separate file which is read by the C preprocessor as instructed by a
directive of the form

```
#include filename
```

The C preprocessor is a good example of how all the variants of an element
can be held within a single source element. [Winkler 88] contains a survey of
the ways in which similar approaches are implemented for other programming languages and environments. Winkler characterises each approach by:

•   The mechanism used to select one of the possible variants. This may be
    by preprocessor directives or by information provided to the pre-
    processor when it is invoked.

- The relationship between the language of the preprocessor directives, the language of the rest of the element before it is preprocessed and the language generated by the preprocessor.

- The extent to which the preprocessor ensures that what it generates is syntactically and semantically correct.

The preprocessing approach is not limited to elements which contain source code for programming languages. Many word processors have a macro facility which allows several variants of a document to be generated from one source. For example, the addressee of a standard letter may be parametrised by a macro so that the letter can be printed with the macro replaced by each of the names in a mailing list.

The functions provided by the C preprocessor are largely independent of the C language. Figure 4.4 illustrates the operation of a general purpose preprocessor which takes as input a multivariant source element and produces variants. The variant elements generated by the preprocessor may be source code, test data, documentation or any other type of text element. These variants are derived elements in the sense described in Section 3.1; although they contain text they should not be changed except by revising the multivariant source element from which they are generated. A general purpose preprocessor only works for source elements which contain plain text; for example, it cannot easily be used to manage variants of diagrams.

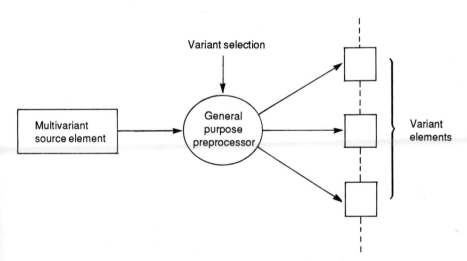

Figure 4.4　A general purpose preprocessor

The power of the multivariant source approach to managing variance lies in the way it solves the double maintenance problem regardless of how the system is structured. Its principal drawbacks are that:

- *Variance is not localised.* If a variant of the system requires small variations of many parts of the system then a change to one variant requires revisions to elements throughout the system.

- *Variants are not separated.* If several variants of an item are represented within a single item then variants cannot be developed and maintained independently. For example, it is not possible to check one variant of the item out of the library without also checking out all the other variants which that item represents.

- *Multivariant items become unreadable.* An element which embodies many variants, in many dimensions, can become so strewn with preprocessor directives that it is hard to understand.

- *It may be necessary to refer to the postprocessed element.* For example, a source level debugger may refer to line numbers of source code after it has been preprocessed. Problems like this arise if the preprocessor is not well integrated with other tools in the environment.

For these reasons the approach should be used as a second line strategy which is particularly useful for small variations which cannot be isolated in separate items. Whenever possible variance should be localised and concentrated.

4.4.4 Multivariant editors

One of the problems noted with storing several variants within a single source element is that the preprocessor directives can confuse the structure of the source element so that it becomes hard to understand. Multivariant editors overcome precisely this problem. To edit a multivariant source element, the user of the editor first selects the *edit set*, which is the set of variants of the item to be edited, and then the *view variant*, which is the element of the edit set which is displayed on the screen. Edit commands issued by the user are applied to all variants in the edit set. Typically the edit set comprises all the permanent variants of an element so that changes can be made to the parts of the element that are common to all variants.

Like the preprocessor approach described in the previous subsection, multivariant editors maintain directives which control which parts of the multivariant source are included in which variants of the element. Unlike the preprocessor approach, these directives are hidden from the user. The editor creates and maintains the directives when the user makes changes to the edit set.

A problem with multivariant editors is that changes are made to variants of elements on the basis of incomplete information. As well as displaying the view variant, multivariant elements also need to show the relationship between the text displayed and variants of the element which are not displayed. The user will probably wish to know which variants of the element a fragment of text belongs to, for example all variants or just the view variant. The user may also wish to know where there are fragments of text which are in some variants, but not the view variant. [Kruskal 84] and [Sarnak 88] describe several approaches for conveying this information using colour, other display attributes and windows; these references also describe experiences developing and using multivariant editors within IBM.

4.5 VERSIONS OF COMPOSITE ITEMS

So far the discussion of item versions has ignored whether an item has components. The principles of version management apply to both composite items and to elements: all items have revisions, temporary and permanent variants, and working versions. There are, however, significant differences in how item versions are managed which arise because a version of a composite item is defined by a version of each of its components.

Figure 4.5 illustrates that the user documentation for the payroll system contains three component elements: an overview, a reference manual and an installation manual. Each of these elements exists as a set of versions. Figure 4.6 shows versions of the user documentation, which are drawn shaded, and of its component elements. The horizontal threads in this figure

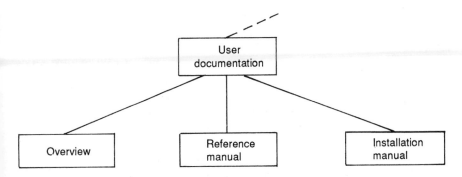

Figure 4.5   The component elements of user documentation

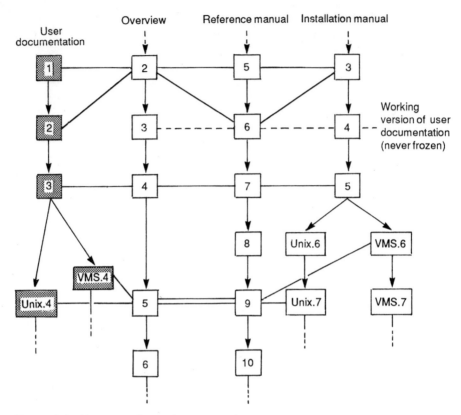

Figure 4.6   Versions of user documentation

define versions of the user documentation by linking together a version of each of its components. Thus version 2 of the user documentation comprises version 2 of the overview, version 6 of the reference manual and version 3 of the installation manual. After version 3, user documentation is needed for each of the Unix and VMS variants of the payroll system; because variance is localised, this only affects the installation manual component.

Note that a new revision of an element does not necessarily require a new revision of an item of which it is a component. Version 3 of the overview does not immediately demand a new version of the user documentation to contain it; in fact version 3 of the overview is not included in any controlled version of the user documentation.

As with elements, composite items evolve through transient working versions. A working version of a composite item may contain both frozen and working versions of its components. The dashed line of Figure 4.6 denotes a working version of the user documentation. This constituted, at some moment, the most recent revision of each component of the user documentation. However, this working version was never frozen.

Defining a version of a composite item is a distinct step from defining versions of its components. Although the components of an item may be correct in themselves, a separate step is needed to approve that the components combine to form a consistent whole; for example, the overview and reference manual in a version of the user documentation must be compatible. In general, a version of an item is established when its components achieve a required level of approval, are mutually consistent and combine to serve a particular purpose. In this way, a new version of an element achieves greater visibility as it is included in items at successively higher levels of the design hierarchy. An item version signals a project milestone; the larger the item, the more significant the milestone.

4.6 DELTA STORAGE

Items exist as a set of similar versions. For the reasons discussed in Section 4.2, all versions of all items must be preserved so they are available when needed. Storing all versions of an item is potentially a very expensive use of disk space. Delta storage is a technique used by CM tools which allows multiple versions of an item to be stored economically.

SCCS [Rochkind 75] provides a simple example of delta storage. The first version of an element is stored as clear text, i.e. fully and explicitly. Version 2 of the element is not stored in full; rather SCCS stores the difference or *delta* between versions 2 and 1. SCCS constructs version 2 of the element when it is needed by applying this delta to version 1. Similarly version 3 is stored as a delta from version 2, and so on.

The delta storage mechanism should be invisible to the user of the CM tool; when the tool is asked to supply a particular version of an element, any processing performed by the tool to construct the version should be entirely hidden from the user. Different tools organise deltas in different ways (see, for example, [Rochkind 75] and [Tichy 85]), but in general deltas bear no relation to the way the versions of the element were actually constructed.

Delta storage dramatically reduces the use of disk space. [Rochkind 75] cites a case study in which SCCS stores a revision of an element in, on average, 10% of the space the element would occupy if stored as clear text. DSEE combines delta storage with blank compression and is thereby able to store an average of 50 to 100 revisions to an element in the space occupied by the element as clear text [Leblang 88].

Few things in life are free. As Tichy remarks in [Tichy 85], the use of deltas is a classic trade-off between space and time: deltas reduce the use of disk space but increase the time to retrieve an element. Using SCCS, the retrieval of the most recent version of an element with many predecessors can be quite slow. RCS's approach to this problem is to store the most recent version of each element as clear text and previous versions as deltas. These deltas are sometimes called backward deltas, in contrast to the forward deltas maintained by SCCS. This approach ensures that recent versions of an element, which are the versions which are usually needed, can be retrieved quickly.

Tools like SCCS, RCS and DSEE provide delta storage for elements. The same principle applies for composite items, and is perhaps even more important. Two versions of a composite item which include the same version of a component item should not cause that component to be stored twice; instead each version should point to the same copy of the component. This is the approach used by most of the CM tools described in later chapters.

4.7 CONFIGURATIONS

A configuration is a collection of elements which fulfil a particular purpose. Typically, a configuration meets the needs of a particular client or environment. For example, a configuration of the payroll system might be assembled to run in France on the Unix operating system.

Formally, a configuration is an item: a collection of elements which are treated as a unit for the purposes of CM. In practice a configuration is usually a large item with few external dependencies. Thus a configuration which includes an element of code will also include other elements that the element uses. The fact that a configuration is self-sufficient in this sense enables it to fulfil its purpose.

A configuration is more general than a design item. Configurations cut across the hierarchy of design items, picking and choosing elements which are needed for the intended purpose. Thus a configuration of the payroll system might exclude all source code and system documentation and will be derived from one variant of each source element. Different configurations may overlap, whereas either two design items are disjoint or one contains the other. There is also a difference of emphasis between a configuration and a design item. For a design item the emphasis is on the source elements it contains. Conversely, the most significant elements of a configuration are often the derived elements, for example, the executable programs. It is often the derived items which actually fulfil the function of a configuration.

This chapter has discussed why variance should be localised in the hierarchy of design items. It has also described how items should be structured so that variants of the item can be developed and maintained. The principal goal has been to eliminate, or at least control, the need to maintain the same software in more than one place.

What has yet to be addressed is how to define and build a particular configuration from an enormous pool of potential elements. In general terms, a configuration is assembled by first defining the source elements to be used to assemble the configuration, then choosing versions of each of these elements and then deriving the configuration. How to control this process is a crucial aspect of CM and is described in subsequent chapters.

Key Points

- The way to modify an item is to check out the item from the software library, change the item and then check in the new version to the library.

- Item versions occur as revisions (which are time-ordered) or as variants (which meet conflicting requirements at the same time).

- Temporary variants are eventually merged into the main line of descent for the item. The longer a temporary variant persists, the harder it is to merge. Tools can help to merge variants, but should not be relied upon.

- Permanent variants are never merged. They arise from varying platforms, varying user requirements and the particular requirements of testing and debugging.

- There are two complementary techniques for managing variance: localising variance within the design item hierarchy and storing many variants within one version of an item which is then processed to give the desired variant.

- Delta storage enables CM tools to store multiple versions of an item efficiently.

5

IDENTIFYING ITEMS

There are two closely related aspects of item identification: designing items and labelling items. Designing items involves structuring software as items which enable configurations of the system to be built and maintained. The first step is to decide what lifecycle model will be used to guide the project and, therefore, what baselines will be produced. The next step is to describe the content of each baseline. Chapter 3 gave guidelines for structuring items within a baseline which take account of management constraints and the need to structure software to minimise dependencies. If a strict top-down design approach is followed, successive phases of the project lifecycle identify levels of the design hierarchy starting at the top and working down. At each level items are identified by their interface.

The second aspect of item identification consists of naming and labelling items in a way that is unambiguous and visible. This aspect provides an antidote to the sort of problems mentioned in Section 1.1 under the heading of item identification:

- A program which ceases to work for no apparent reason.

- Debugging an executable program by referring to an incompatible listing of the source code.

- Failure to reproduce a program fault which has been reported in the field.

- Uncertainty as to whether or not a change has been made to a program.

It is this second aspect of item identification which is the subject of this chapter. The assumption is that all project software has been structured as items; the question now is how these items are to be described.

5.1 NAMING ITEMS

Every item must have a *name* that identifies it uniquely. Establishing a naming scheme for items must be one of the first tasks of CM planning. For most purposes, the most effective naming scheme makes use of the hierarchy of design items described in Chapter 3. Each item in the hierarchy is given a name which distinguishes it from other items with the same parent. Thus, for a three-level hierarchy an element would have a three-part name:

```
system / subsystem / element
```

The last part of the name of an item is called its *relative name*; all the elements of one subsystem must have different relative names. The hierarchical directory structures used by operating systems use precisely this approach to name files.

There are two conflicting requirements for how the name of an item should be chosen: that the name should be succinct and that it should be descriptive. At the former extreme, items are identified by a serial number; this approach is sometimes used by large military projects with very formal CM controls. If a naming scheme produces short and therefore cryptic names, then items may be given an alternative informal title. Documents are sometimes identified in this way; for example, this book is formally identified as ISBN 0 471 92940 9 but it also has a title which is more informative and longer.

Beware of numeric naming schemes which give no clue to an item's content. They rarely work. Recall the DBMS system illustrated in Figure 3.1. In theory the Optimise element could be identified as DBMS/3/2 where 3 means the third subsystem (Query Processing) and 2 means the second element in that subsystem. This is fine in theory; however, it does not help a programmer who wishes to examine the Optimise element but does not know its position in the hierarchy. Good CM should provide a less user hostile way of naming items!

For all the software engineering environments described in this book, elements correspond to files maintained by the host operating system. CM tools which manage a software library check out an element from the library by creating a file in the developer's private workspace that contains that element. The relative name of the file is the same as the relative name of the element. For example, the CMS command

```
RESERVE MYPACKAGE.ADA
```

checks out (in CMS terminology RESERVEs) the element MYPACKAGE.ADA from the CMS library to a file of that name in the user's current default directory. A consequence of this is that CM tools restrict the relative name of an element to be a valid filename of the operating system platform. Usually this prohibits embedded spaces in the name and limits its length.

Often the content of an element suggests its relative name in a very direct way. For example, it is both natural and descriptive to derive the name of an element which contains a single FORTRAN subroutine from the name of the subroutine. Thus an element containing a subroutine called SORT would have a relative name of SORT.FOR. The .FOR extension indicates the type of element: FORTRAN source code. Other extensions indicate related elements; thus SORT.O and SORT.LIST contain the object code and compiler listing which are derived from SORT.FOR by the FORTRAN compiler. Extensions are a very effective way of advertising to both people and tools what the element contains. CM must classify elements by their type and define the extension to be used for each type.

The example of the FORTRAN subroutine raises the question of whether it is really sensible to allow two elements of different subsystems to have the same relative name. Suppose there is a second, and quite different, subroutine called SORT in another subsystem. Suppose also that the two subsystems are linked together in a single executable program. Some linkers detect this sort of clash and flag an error, others some simply ignore one of the subroutines, with horrific consequences! To avoid this problem CM must ensure that when a new element is named there is not already a subroutine of that name which might be linked with the new subroutine. There are two approaches to the problem: the first is to use a naming convention which precludes the possibility of clashes; the second is to maintain a list of names and their scope and to check that each new name does not already appear in the list. Name clash problems, and their solution, vary greatly with the type of item. For example, files containing several C functions, Ada units and elements which define screen layouts all have different referencing and scoping rules which require different naming strategies to avoid clashes.

Whatever strategy is used to name items, it is important that it is defined and enforced at an early stage of a software development project. The ability to name something is the first step towards being able to manage it.

5.2 IDENTIFYING VERSIONS OF ITEMS

5.2.1 Identifying revisions

As discussed in Chapter 4, items evolve through a succession of revisions. Each revision of an item needs to be distinguished from all other revisions. The simplest way to identify a revision is with a single integer. When an item is first identified it is revision 1; subsequent revisions are 2, 3, 4, etc.

Many CM tools, for example CMS, DSEE and CCC, use this simple and effective numbering scheme. The revision number of an item is automatically incremented when the item is checked into the software library.

Some tools, for example SCCS and RCS, identify a revision of an element with a pair of integers, sometimes called the release number and the level number. Figure 5.1 shows a succession of revisions of an RCS element.

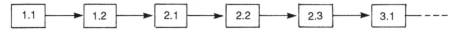

Figure 5.1   Successive revisions in RCS

A change to the release number, for example between revisions 2.3 and 3.1 in Figure 5.1, is used to indicate a major change to the item. What constitutes a major change varies with the type of item. For an item with a well-defined interface, a new release may signal a change to that interface. For an item of user documentation, a new release may signal a substantial rather than cosmetic change. For items near the top of the design hierarchy, which are visible to users of the system, revision numbers may be influenced as much by marketing as by technical considerations.

Using the date to identify a revision is not usually recommended. There are three principal problems:

- Two revisions of an item may need to be created on the same day.

- The identification is cumbersome, especially if time is also included in the identification to solve the first problem.

- A date gives no clue to the identity of the previous or next revision of the item.

5.2.2 Identifying permanent variants

Recall that an item may exist as a set of variants for each of several dimensions of variance. The payroll system described in Chapter 4 has two dimensions of variance: the operating system platform and the country where the payroll system is to be used. There are therefore two enumerated types which describe the variance of an item in the payroll system:

Country: US, UK, FRANCE, GERMANY
Operating system : UNIX, VMS, OS/2

Each item potentially exists as a set of $12 = 4 \times 3$ variants: one for each combination of country and operating system.

A simple and effective way of identifying a variant of an item is to append the variant name for each dimension of variance to the name of the item. If an item is the same for all the variants in a dimension then nothing is appended to the name for that dimension. Thus a variant of an item X to run in France on VMS is identified as X.FRANCE.VMS; a variant of Y which is independent of country but specific to Unix is identified as X.UNIX.

5.2.3 Identifying temporary variants

Temporary variants may also be identified by adding a suffix to the name of the item. In DSEE the name of a temporary variant follows the name of the element and a /; the revision number for the element is enclosed in square brackets. Figure 5.2 illustrates versions of a DSEE element called X which has a temporary variant called FIX.

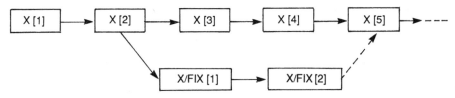

Figure 5.2   Identifying temporary variants using DSEE

A problem with this identification strategy is that the temporary variant name FIX cannot be reused, at least not for temporary variants of X; if it were, the identification X/FIX[1] would be ambiguous. A naming convention is needed to ensure that one element does not have two branches of the same name. The DSEE case study in Chapter 8 illustrates just such a convention.

CMS and RCS use a different approach to identifying versions which gets round this problem. These tools include the version identifier of the base item for a temporary variant in the version identifier of the variant. Figure 5.3 shows the version identifiers for a tree of RCS elements. Recall that RCS identifies revisions using two integers. Version 3.2.1.1 is the first revision of a temporary variant of version 3.2; versions 3.2.1.2, 3.2.1.3 and 3.2.2.1 are successive revisions of this variant.

The problem with this scheme is that version identifiers can become very complicated, especially if there are variants of variants, as in Figure 5.3.

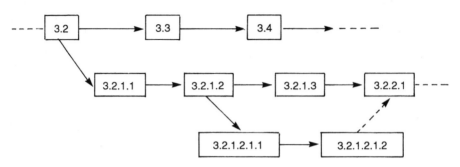

Figure 5.3   Identifying temporary variants using RCS

Furthermore, the numeric version identifiers allow no way of indicating the reason for the temporary variant. The simple approach exemplified by DSEE is better in most circumstances.

5.3 DESCRIBING AN ITEM'S DERIVATION

As well as assigning every item in the system a unique identifier it is also invaluable to associate further information with the item which describes how it was produced. If a problem is detected with a new version of a program it is essential to be able to answer the following questions:

- Which versions of which source elements were used to build the program?
- What tools and options were used to process these source elements?
- Which source elements have been revised since the previous version of the program was built?
- How have the source elements been changed, and why?
- Have all the source elements for the program been tested and approved?
- Have the tools used to build the program changed?

These are the first questions that a programmer should ask when confronted with a fault which is any way mysterious or unexpected. It is the job of CM to provide precise and reliable answers to these questions. Many programmer hours have been wasted studying the intricacies of code because the answers were either not known or not carefully reviewed.

This section describes the minimal information which must be associated with each item; the next section describes how this information can be recorded. In each of these sections source and derived items are discussed separately.

5.3.1 The change history of source items

All source items must have an associated *change history* which describes how and why a revision of an item differs from its predecessors. This description should include at least the date the item was revised, who was responsible for the revision and why the item was changed. Chapter 9 describes how changes to approved items correspond to change requests; the change history for an item should refer to the change requests which the new version of the item implements.

Every source item should also have a status attribute which defines the level of approval which the item has achieved. The range of status values for an element of code might be untested, module tested and integration tested; for a document the values might be draft, proposed and approved.

5.3.2 The derivation of derived elements

A derived element is, by definition, constructed by processing other elements, both source and derived. The derivation of a derived element is fully described by:

- The full identification, i.e. the name and the version, of each of the source elements from which the derived element is directly built.

- The derivation of each of the derived elements from which the derived element is directly built.

- The full identification of the tool used to build the derived element.

- The options passed to the tool to build the derived element, for example the options passed to a compiler.

- The date and time when the tool was used to build the derived element.

Note that this description is recursive. It involves scanning down a tree of derived elements until the leaf source elements are identified. Figure 5.4 is a simple example of such a tree.

The derivation of PROG is described by the derivation of A.O and B.O, the identification of the Linker and the Linker options used to build PROG; the derivation of A.O (respectively B.O) is described by the full identification of A.C (respectively B.C), the compiler and the options passed to the compiler.

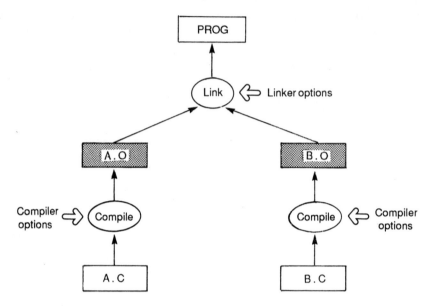

Figure 5.4   A simple derivation tree

In many cases the order in which intermediate derived elements are built is either unimportant or obvious. In Figure 5.4 there are three processing steps: two compilations and one link. The link step cannot take place until both source elements have been compiled, and the order of compilation is irrelevant. In an old-fashioned 'compile and link' environment the order in which derived items are built is not usually an issue.

Conversely, for many modern tools the order in which source elements are processed is crucial. A data dictionary is typically constructed by processing source elements which add information to the dictionary. Data structures, form layouts and procedures written in a fourth generation language are successively added into the dictionary. The order of the steps which build the dictionary is often critical and not obvious; for example, a data structure must be defined in the dictionary before it is referenced.

The Ada language achieves type checking between separately compiled units by requiring that the specification part of all units used by an Ada unit is compiled before the unit itself is compiled. Chapter 8 will describe the consequences of this requirement; clearly these include that the order of compilation is highly significant.

One way of recording the order of the processing steps which built a derived element is to record the time of each step. This attribute can also help to resolve any uncertainty about the state of the software engineering environment when the element was built.

A more methodical approach is to describe the derivation of a derived element by:

- The full identifiers of all source elements used to construct the derived element either directly or indirectly.

- The full identifiers of all the tools used to construct the derived element from the source elements.

- A description of how the tools are used to construct the derived element from the source elements, including the options passed to the tool and, where significant, the order of the processing steps.

The third part of this description is provided by the system model. The system model is a source item which describes how items are transformed by tools into derived items. Like other items the system model exists in different versions: the system model is revised as the structure of the system evolves and variants of the system are described by variant system models. With this approach, the derivation of PROG in Figure 5.4 is described by the full identification of A.C, B.C, the compiler, the linker and the system model. The next three chapters describe different ways of organising the system model which are provided by different CM tools and are suitable for different types of item.

5.4 RECORDING AN ELEMENT'S IDENTITY AND DERIVATION

Previous sections of this chapter have discussed information associated with an element: its identification and its derivation. How and where should this information be held? Consider again some of the questions to which item identification must provide answers:

- What has changed in this element?
- Which version of the program is this?
- Does this listing correspond to this program?

The recurrence of the word 'this' in these questions suggests that the information about an element should be tightly coupled to the element itself, so that the information is available when and where it is needed.

The best place to hold information about an element is as part of the element itself. It is usually possible to describe a text source element within the element: a document may have a front sheet which formally identifies the document and describes its history; an element of source code may include comments which describe how it has evolved. Describing a derived element within the element is often more difficult. This section describes methods and tools for recording an item's identity and derivation visibly and reliably.

5.4.1 Source elements

Many CM tools automatically maintain information about elements of source text within the element. SCCS [Rochkind 75] provides a set of *identification keywords,* each of which corresponds to information which identifies the item. The keyword M corresponds to the (relative) name of the element, I corresponds to its version and G to the date the element was created. When an SCCS element is checked out of the library any keyword which is enclosed between two % characters is expanded to the corresponding identifying information in the working version of the element. For example, the following line might be part of a source element held by SCCS, perhaps within the header of the element:

Element relative name = %M%; Version = %I%; Date created = %G%

When the element is checked out of the library, SCCS expands the keywords to give, for example:

Element relative name = prog.c; Version = 2.3; Date created = May 23 1991

A limitation of SCCS's approach is that an element should not be checked into the library after keywords have been expanded. SCCS's only help with this problem is to provide an option on its check out command which specifies whether or not keywords are expanded. A check out which is the first step in revising the element would not normally expand keywords; a check out which fetches elements from the library to build a configuration of the system would expand keywords. Unfortunately, keyword expansion is often desirable even if the element is to be revised.

RCS [Tichy 85] provides a neater solution to the problem. Keywords are always expanded when the element is checked out of the library, but the expansion leaves a trace of the unexpanded keyword in the source element. For example, the text

%I%

is expanded by RCS to

%I: 1.1 %

when revision 1.1 of the element is checked out. If the element is then checked in to the RCS library as revision 1.2, then the next time the element is checked out, RCS changes the text to

%I: 1.2 %

Some CM tools, including SCCS, RCS and CMS, provide other facilities for recording the history of an element. Whenever a new version of an element is checked into the library, the engineer gives a summary of the change that has been made. As well as remembering the summary description, the CM tool can add it to a change history which is maintained within the element. The CM tool must either know or be told where in the file the history is to be maintained and how the history should be formatted so that it is treated as a comment by other tools which process the element.

The following is an example of a change history maintained by CMS:

```
--      Change history for DATE.ADA
--
-- *4     July 15 1991     18:31     JCW
-- Merge FIX temporary variant into rewrite (CR 185)
--
-- *3     July 1 1991      16:45     JCW
-- Rewrite for dates in US or UK format (CR 180)
--
-- FIX.2  May 3 1991       02:13     SHB
-- Cater for hiatus at end of centuries (CR 193)
--
-- FIX.1  May 2 1991       23:15     SHB
-- Urgent fix for leap years (CR 191)
--
-- *2     April 8 1991     11:46     KVR
-- Pack dates into a single integer (CR 102)
-- Correct end condition in the for loop
-- through months (CR 93)
--
-- *1     March 25 1991    10:15     KVR
-- First version of subprogram to convert a date to
-- text as required by the report generator
--
--      End of change history
```

It comprises a series of entries, one for each version of the element. Entries are in reverse chronological order, which reflects their relative importance. Each entry describes the version number of the element, the date and time the element was checked into the library, who checked in the element and a summary of how the element has been changed. Here the version identifiers which are on the main line of descent are preceded by an *. Each change summary includes a reference to the change request (CR) which the new version implements; change requests are discussed in detail in Chapter 9.

Some CM tools annotate source elements to indicate which lines have been added or changed in which versions of the element. For example, CMS optionally appends --x to a line of Ada which was last modified in version x of the element. All lines which have been modified since the first version of the element are annotated in this way. The annotation can be related to the change history to determine when, why and by whom the modification was made. The technique is an extension of the idea of change bars which are commonly used to highlight amendments to documents.

It is to some extent a matter of taste whether the change history is held as part of the element, provided that the change history is recorded somewhere. All the CM tools mentioned in this section have commands which elicit the change history of an element. For example, the command

```
sccs    prt    date.ada    -r4.1
```

elicits the change history for version 4.1 of date.ada. If a CM tool does not record an element's change history, then a document like the change history, shown above needs to be maintained manually, preferably within the element. On the other hand, it is folly to maintain manually information that is also held by a CM tool; the manual and automated records will inevitably diverge and confusion will abound.

5.4.2 Derived elements

To answer questions like 'What version of the program is this?' and 'How does this version of the program differ from the previous version?' requires knowledge of which source elements were used to build the program and which tools were used. As with source elements, it is a good principle to record information about a derived element within the element itself; however, the way this principle is put into practice is quite different for derived elements.

It is not usually possible to identify a version of a derived element in terms of the versions of source elements from which it is built. Suppose version 7 of DATE.ADA is compiled into an object module, DATE.O. It might be argued that the derived element should be identified as version 7 of

DATE.O. Unfortunately this identification does not account for the options passed to the Ada compiler to build the object module: suppose version 7 of DATE.ADA is recompiled with different options. How should this derived element be identified? The confusion becomes worse when the derived element is built from many sources.

The version identification of a derived element must distinguish it from other instances of the same element but it does not, in itself, describe its derivation. For example, a version of the executable program of the payroll system might be identified as version Unix.3. Some other mechanism is needed to determine precisely how the program was derived.

A description of how a derived element was built cannot be included within the element as a comment in the way described for source elements. For one thing, a derived element is very often a binary file to which text cannot be added. Furthermore, editing a derived element to include its derivation breaks the rule that a derived element is built by automatic processing of other elements.

A partial solution to this problem is to include the identity of a source element within the source in such a way that it is inherited by elements which are derived from it. For example, SCCS keyword parameters may be included in C, PL/1 and Pascal code as, respectively:

```
static char SccsId[ ] = "%W% %I%"
DCL SCCSID CHAR(20) INIT('%W% %I%')
CONST SCCSID = '%W% %I%'
```

The keyword parameters are expanded by SCCS when the source element is checked out of the library. The identifiers are then embedded in object modules and executable programs when the source element is compiled and linked. The problem then is to find these identifiers when they are needed! The %W% keyword in the above examples is expanded by SCCS to a special string of characters followed by the name of the element. The 'sccs what' command searches an element for the special string; the element identifiers which follow each occurrence of this string are then reported as the source elements from which the element was built.

This is a very useful trick but a rather clumsy one. The procedure can be subverted by compilers which optimise code (and notice that constants like SCCSID are never used and therefore ignore them); it must also be used carefully when identifying include files (to avoid defining the same constant twice). Further, the structure of the derived element is being used for a purpose for which it was not intended. Some operating systems (as well as environments like PCTE) provide slots which are designed to hold information about derived elements.

Many CM tools record information about a derived element in a way which is tightly coupled to the element, although not actually part of the element. For example, DSEE maintains an associated Bound Configuration Thread (BCT) for each derived element. The BCT describes the tools that were used to derive the item, the options with which the tools were invoked and the source elements; see Chapter 8 for further details. A problem with this approach is that when a derived item is issued from the CM tool, for example for distribution to a client, the link to the element's derivation is cut. The way to manage this problem is to make sure that the identity of the derived element is manifest and that it points unambiguously to the description of how the element was derived. For example, the payroll system might have built into it a command which causes the program to identify itself. When a user discovers a fault in the program he or she uses this command to determine that, say, version Unix.3 of the program is being used. This version identification then enables whoever investigates the fault to determine precisely how the program was derived. Unix.3 might identify a particular DSEE BCT, or it might identify a configuration which contains all the source elements that were used to build the program.

5.5 IDENTIFYING CONFIGURATIONS

The difference between an element and a configuration is that a configuration is a composite item; its content is precisely the list of its components. Recall the versions of the user documentation illustrated by Figure 4.6. Version Unix.4 of the user documentation comprises version 5 of the overview, version 9 of the reference manual and version Unix.7 of the installation manual.

How are configurations formally identified and where should this identification be recorded? This section summarises manual and tool based approaches to this question. The approaches are described in much greater detail by subsequent chapters.

5.5.1 Using a form to identify configurations

Versions of a composite item may be identified using a paper form which records the components of the item. Figure 5.5 is an example of such a form. The form, sometimes called a *Version Description Document*, or *VDD*, has been filled in to describe version Unix.4 of the user documentation shown in Figure 4.6.

The information about a composite item is similar to that recorded about an element. The difference is that the content of a composite item is a list of the items it contains. Of course the components enumerated in a VDD may themselves be composite, and therefore described by separate VDDs.

Version Description Document	
Item: User documentation	
Part of: Payroll system	
Version: Unix. 4	
Status: Approved | *By:* FJC | *Date:* 5 November 1990	
Description: First Unix variant of user documentation	
Implements CRs: 77,81	
Component	*Version*
Overview Reference manual Installation manual	5 9 Unix.7

Figure 5.5   Identifying components with a VDD

Similarly, the complete payroll system has its own VDD which includes user documentation among its components. Paper VDDs are often used to identify the release of a configuration to a client; the documentation which needs to accompany a release is discussed further in Chapter 11.

5.5.2 Using tools to identify configurations

The simplest approach to identifying a configuration is to store all its components in one place. For software items this means that all components are held in one directory of the operating system directory structure. Further details of this simple approach are given in Chapter 6.

CMS and DSEE both enable a composite item to be defined as a collection of elements. Neither of these tools provide a multilevel structure in which a composite item can itself contain composite items. A CMS class contains one version of each element covered by the class. Any CMS command which takes an element, or set of elements, as an argument may identify an element version by referring to a class to which the element belongs. For example, if a CMS class is used to hold all element versions which are being integration tested, then a single CMS command checks out all the elements of this class.

In DSEE a list of element versions is defined by a configuration thread. Metaphorically, a thread is a piece of string which links together instances of elements to form a configuration; the horizontal lines of Figure 4.6 are threads. DSEE enables a configuration to be defined by rules which select which element versions are linked by a thread. For example, version Unix.4 of the user documentation might be specified as:

Select the same version of each element as is used in VMS.4, unless the element has a branch called Unix, in which case use the most recent version of this branch.

DSEE's facilities for defining configuration threads are closely related to its facilities for building derived elements. This aspect of CM is the subject of the next three chapters. In particular, Chapter 7 describes DSEE in detail, including the syntax used to define a configuration thread.

CMS and DSEE provide comparatively low level facilities which can be used to support a range of different approaches to CM. It is left to the CMS user to make effective use of the CMS class facility. Tools like CCC/DM and Lifespan go further towards providing a complete CM environment for developing and maintaining software. For example, CCC/DM provides configurations for versions of elements which are under development, under test, approved and in production. The way elements are promoted through these four configurations is closely related to CCC/DM's change lifecycle, which is described in Chapter 10.

Key Points

- Each item must be named in a way which distinguishes it from other items. Each version of an item must be identified so that it is distinguished from other versions.

- The most effective ways of naming items use the structure of the design item hierarchy. The name of an item should also indicate its content.

- The identification of an item must include its approval status and a description of how the item was produced.

- A derived item is described by the source items and tools used to build it. The change history of a source item describes how it differs from other versions of the item.

- The record of an item's identity should be closely coupled with the item itself so that it is available when and where it is needed.

6

DEFINING AND BUILDING CONFIGURATIONS

This chapter describes methods and tools for defining and building configurations. Recall that a configuration is a collection of elements which fulfil a particular purpose, for example a version of a payroll system which runs on a particular operating system and is suitable for a particular country. A configuration is a more general composite item than a design item; configurations cut across the design hierarchy, picking and choosing the elements which enable the configuration to fulfil its purpose. The components of a configuration are ultimately a collection of element names and versions. Thus a configuration may be defined with a simple form such as Figure 5.5. In practice, it is often more useful to define a configuration indirectly in terms of the properties of its components.

Chapter 5 concentrated on identifying composite items which consist of source elements. In general, configurations contain derived elements. Indeed, it is the derived elements, such as executable programs, which typically fulfil the configuration's intended purpose. The identification of a composite item which includes derived elements must define both the component source elements and the way the source elements are transformed into derived elements by tools. CM must ensure that the derived elements are built accurately and efficiently.

This chapter describes more sophisticated techniques for selecting source elements for a configuration than simple enumeration. It also addresses the crucial question of how to control the way in which derived items are built.

71

6.1 PRINCIPLES

Figure 6.1 shows the inputs and outputs of the process of defining and building a configuration. The inputs to the process are:

- *The source elements.* The raw material from which the configuration is built.

- *The system model.* A description of the relationship between the elements which are needed to build the required configuration, in particular how tools are used to build derived elements from source elements.

- *Version selection.* A selection of the element versions which are to be used to build the configuration.

- *Derived elements.* A pool of derived elements which, for some reason, have already been built and therefore do not need to be rebuilt.

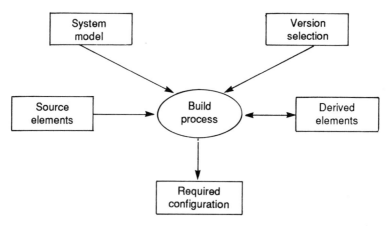

Figure 6.1   Defining and building a configuration

The outputs of the build process are the required configuration and, as a by-product, derived elements which can be added to the pool and used to build other configurations. This section discusses the principles of this process. Subsequent sections, and the next two chapters, describe in detail how these principles are implemented by different CM environments.

6.1.1 The system model

The representation of a system model varies between CM environments. The simplest and the most commonly used representation is a *build command file*: a procedural description of the processing steps which build all the derived elements of a configuration from the source elements. On an IBM mainframe a command file might be written in JCL; under Unix it is likely to be a shell script. The configuration is built by simply executing the command file.

The Unix tool Make uses a more concise representation of a system's structure which is declarative rather than procedural. Make's system model is a called a Makefile; by examining the Makefile, the Make program determines what processing steps are required and in what order they should be performed. Make has built-in knowledge of the more obvious dependencies between elements. For example, Make knows that the way to process an element with a name which ends in .PAS is to compile the element using the Pascal compiler. Because this knowledge is implicit in the Make tool it does not need to be made explicit in the Makefile. More sophisticated tools than Make deduce dependencies between elements based upon their content rather than simply their name; see, for example, the description of Odin in [Clemm 88].

6.1.2 Versions

A common feature of all approaches to system modelling is that the model does not refer to specific item versions. For example, Section 3.2 listed the following build command file to compile and link a program called ACOMP:

```
ASSEMBLE    LEX.ASS
CCOMPILE    PARSER.C
CCOMPILE    CODEGEN.C
LINK PARSER.O, LEX.O, CODEGEN.O EXE=ACOMP
```

This command file is a system model for the ACOMP system. It identifies elements by name and does not qualify the name with a version identifier. The rationale for this generality is clear: the system model remains constant through many revisions of the system. Of course, the system model must change if the structure of the system changes. For example, if CODEGEN.C becomes too large it may be split into two elements; the system model will then need to be revised accordingly. To manage such changes, the system model must itself be managed as an item just like source code and documentation. On the other hand, the system model does not and should not change with every revision to the elements to which it refers.

To define a configuration a specific version must be selected for each of the items in the model. The following are some of the reasons why alternative configurations may be needed:

- To build variants of the system to meet the requirements of different clients or different environments.

- To rebuild versions of the system which are in operational use, for example to investigate an operational fault.

- To enable a developer to work in the context of a frozen configuration, immune from the activity of other developers.

- To allow a set of revisions to be included in a configuration when, but only when, they have been approved as a consistent set.

Each of these configurations requires a particular selection of source elements. Different CM environments use different approaches for selecting element versions. Used on their own, neither build command files nor Makefiles provide much assistance for version selection. Both use versions of elements which are in a particular place—in the case of the command file listed above, the default directory. Other methods and tools are needed to ensure that the required element versions find their way to this place.

The simplest approach to version selection is to maintain what amounts to an explicit list of element versions. More sophisticated approaches enable versions to be selected on the basis of their properties and their mutual compatibility. For example, a configuration might be defined to include the most recent tested version of each item or to include the most recent version of each item on a certain date.

6.1.3 Incremental building

Building all the derived items required for a configuration can be a very expensive process in terms of machine resources. A large system may contain many thousands of elements of source code, each of which must be compiled and then linked into an executable program. If just one of the source elements is changed there is no need to recompile the others in order to link a new version of the executable program. This simple economy is an example of the technique of incremental building: when building a configuration use existing derived items where possible.

As Figure 6.1 indicates, the process of assembling a configuration involves both building new derived items and using existing derived items which are suitable for the required configuration. It is often far from obvious which derived elements need to be rebuilt when some but not all of the source elements change. The blanket approach of rebuilding all derived items is uneconomical. On the other hand, failure to rebuild an element which should be rebuilt can be disastrous. If a file of constant declarations is changed and some, but not all, of the source elements in which this file is included are recompiled the resulting program will use inconsistent values of the constants. Tracking down the problems which may ensue is precisely the sort of nightmare that CM seeks to avoid.

Make was perhaps the first CM tool to address the problem of controlling the processing needed to build a configuration. As Feldman remarks in [Feldman 79], 'It (Make) was originally written because its author kept forgetting to compile parts of programs before loading them together.' Make is, however, by no means the last word on the subject of tools which control the construction of derived elements. Tools such as DSEE and the Rational Environment use much more sophisticated rules for deciding when a derived element needs to be rebuilt. To give a simple example of such a rule, the Rational Environment recognises that an Ada unit does not need to be recompiled if the only change to the unit is to add a comment.

6.2 USING BASIC OPERATING SYSTEM FACILITIES

This section examines techniques for defining and building configurations using only those facilities which are provided by most operating systems. Two such facilities are particularly useful in this context: command files and a hierarchical directory structure. Command files allow operating system commands which build derived items to be held in a file which can be configuration managed as a source element; such a command file is called a *build command file*. A directory structure allows the same, or similar, command files to be executed in the context of different directories to build different configurations.

Extensive use of operating system facilities can provide quite sophisticated CM environments which rival the environments provided by commercial CM tools. Rather than describe how to use command files to construct a tool like CCC, this section concentrates on how simple mechanisms can be used to provide simple but effective CM environments suitable for small or medium sized projects.

6.2.1 Build command files

A build command file contains operating system commands which construct derived elements. There is a great danger that a build command file grows as software evolves but is never properly designed. A build command file may have a simple structure for the initial version of a system. By the time the system is finally released to users different elements of source code are compiled with different options, bottlenecks in the system have been rewritten in assembler and several variants of the system are required. Unless active efforts are made to the contrary, the build command file will by then have become unstructured and hard to maintain.

Like all programs a build command file must be carefully designed. Related processing steps should be grouped together and identical processing steps on different elements should be executed by the same command file fragment. Command languages often have basic structuring facilities such as selection and iteration constructs and subroutines. It must be admitted, however, that many command languages do not encourage the writing of well-structured build command files.

There are three guidelines for writing and structuring build command files: parametrise, automate and manage errors.

Parametrise

A single build command file can and should be used to assemble variant configurations. The command file is invoked with one or more parameters which define the characteristics of the derived items. As an example, consider the requirement to build configurations for debugging and for operational use. The only difference between the processing steps which build these two configurations is the options passed to the compiler and linker. Whether a debug or operational configuration is assembled should be determined by a parameter passed to the build command file.

There are several techniques which can be used to parametrise a build command file. Most command languages provide variables which can be used to determine the flow of control through a command file. Many command languages provide a macro facility by which macro variables are replaced with their current values before a command line is executed; for example, the command line

```
PASCAL SORT option
```

would compile SORT with the options currently set in the macro variable called *option*. Another technique is to preprocess a build command file using a general purpose preprocessor of the kind described in Section 4.4.3.

The most effective way to parametrise a build command file depends on the facilities offered by the command language. Whatever techniques are used, the objective is to allow variant configurations to be assembled easily, without maintaining several similar build command files.

Automate

Build command files should define precisely and completely how derived elements are constructed; as little as possible should be left to manual intervention. The ideal model for a build command file is that an engineer supplies parameters for the build, these parameters are validated by the command file which then constructs the required configuration without further intervention by the engineer. This approach allows the build command file to be executed as a background or batch job.

To be avoided is a build command file which requires frequent manual intervention, for example to run a series of command files in the correct order. As well as wasting the engineer's time, this approach demands too much expertise from the engineer. The first objective of build command files is to automate the construction of derived items as completely as possible. The knowledge of how to build configurations must not be buried in the head of a single member of the project team.

Manage errors

A build command file must cater for errors during the execution of the build. Errors may be caused by faults in the elements being processed, for example compilation errors, or a problem in the environment, for example the disk which is to hold the configuration becomes full.

A build command file must ensure that:

• If an error occurs, the build command file detects the error and responds accordingly. Depending on the nature of the error the appropriate response may be to abandon the build, to ignore the error or to continue the build but with a less ambitious objective such as checking the syntax of the source code without generating the object code.

• All errors are recorded. The build command file should leave an audit trail which records exactly what happened during each processing step of the build.

• An error during the build does not compromise existing configurations which will be needed if the build fails. For example, a build which overwrites the derived elements in an old configuration and then fails produces a set of inconsistent derived elements, some from the old configuration and some from the new. All derived elements should be safely backed up before a build so that these elements can be recovered if they are needed.

6.2.2 Using directories to hold configurations

The best directory structure to hold configurations varies with the amount of software to be managed and the phase of the software in its lifecycle. Figure 6.2 shows a simple directory structure which is suitable for holding configurations of a small system and comprises no more than ten thousand lines of source elements.

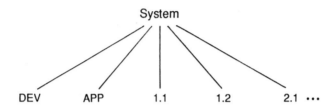

Figure 6.2   A directory structure suitable for a small system

The DEV directory contains the most recent revision of all elements in the system. When an element is to be revised it is checked out of this directory, updated in the developer's working directory and then checked back in to the DEV directory.

Once an element has been tested and approved, perhaps by an independent quality control authority, it is copied from the DEV directory to the APP directory. The APP directory contains the most recent revision of each element which has been approved.

From time to time, for example when the approved configuration of the system is released to users, the APP directory is copied to another directory. These are the directories 1.1, 1.2, 2.1, ... shown in Figure 6.2; the directory 2.1 contains version 2.1 of the system. Note that the DEV and APP directories contain configurations which evolve as elements are checked into the development configuration and then promoted to the approved configuration. On the other hand, the 1.1, 1.2, 2.1,... directories are defined as snapshots of the approved configuration and are frozen from the moment they are defined.

The build command file selects the version of an element which is in the same directory as the command file itself; this allows the same build command file to be used to build each of the configurations shown in Figure 6.2. On the other hand, the build command file may be invoked with different parameters for different configurations; for example, the development configuration might be built with 'debug' options.

The directories shown in Figure 6.2 contain all the source and derived elements of the different configurations of the system. When a source element is included in the development or approved configuration all elements which are derived from the new revision, either directly or indirectly, must be rebuilt. When should these derived elements be rebuilt? There are two simple strategies: the first is to rebuild all the derived elements which depend upon a source element whenever a new version of the source element is added to a configuration; the second is periodically to rebuild the complete configuration from its source elements, for example overnight.

One obvious deficiency of the approach outlined above is that when an element is checked into the DEV directory the previous revision is overwritten; unless the old revision happens to be included in one of the other configurations it is lost forever. This contradicts a basic principle of version management, namely that items should not be revised such that the previous content of the item is lost. A simple solution to this problem is to maintain an archive directory which contains all versions of all source elements. Whenever a new revision is checked into the DEV directory, it is also copied to the archive directory. In this directory, the version identification of the element is incorporated in the name of the file containing the element; for example, version 3.4 of SORT.PAS could be archived in a file called SORT_3_4.PAS.

6.2.3 Search paths for experimental builds

Consider the requirements of an engineer who needs to revise an element of code, say SORT.PAS. She checks the latest revision of the element out of the development configuration and makes changes to the code in her working directory. How is the engineer to assemble experimental versions of the system to test the changes before checking the new revision back into the development configuration?

The simplest solution is to check out all the elements needed to test SORT.PAS, even though none of these elements needs to be revised. This amounts to taking a snapshot of the development configuration which then provides a context for testing changes to SORT.PAS.

A better solution is to allow read access to elements in the development configuration which may then be used to build experimental versions of the system. As an example of this approach, suppose that the LINK step which builds the executable program is LINK *.O, i.e. link together all object modules (files with a suffix of .O). To test changes made to SORT.PAS requires that the system is built using SORT.O from the engineer's working directory and other object modules from the DEV directory.

Many operating systems provide a search path facility which can be used to achieve this without copying all object modules into one directory. The LINK tool first looks for object modules in the current default directory (the engineer's working directory); it then looks for object modules in other directories as specified by a search path. In this case the search path would direct the LINK tool to the DEV directory. Alternatively, should the engineer wish to test changes with the approved or a frozen configuration the search path can be set accordingly.

6.2.4 A directory structure for subsystems

The directory structure shown in Figure 6.2 is flat: it does not partition software elements into design items in the way discussed in Chapter 3. Figure 6.3 extends the directory structure of Figure 6.2 by dividing the system into subsystems. Three subsystems are shown in Figure 6.3: DB, UI and MAIN.

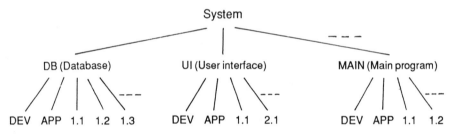

Figure 6.3   A directory structure for subsystems

In this structure each subsystem has its own development, approved and frozen configurations. Different subsystems may be the responsibility of different people, or teams of people, and each can evolve separately. This type of directory structure is suitable for medium sized software systems which comprise a few hundred thousand lines of source elements.

The system model is described by build command files for each subsystem. Each build command file typically constructs:

- Intermediate derived elements, such as object modules, for each source element in the subsystem.
- Executable programs, both test programs and programs which form part of the delivered system, which are linked from object modules in this and other subsystems.

In general, a subsystem uses software in other subsystems to build its executable programs. Build command files must therefore reference derived elements of other subsystems. The directory structure of Figure 6.3 allows a choice of which version of each other subsystem is used. For example, the test program for the DB subsystem might use features of the UI subsystem which are under development but have not yet been approved; the program should therefore be built using object modules from the DEV directory of UI. On the other hand, a version of an executable program in the MAIN subsystem which is part of a released configuration should be frozen; it should therefore be built using frozen configurations of DB and UI.

The build command file should be parametrised so that the choice of subsystem version is made just once. The assignment of these parameters should be kept separate from the processing steps where the parameters are used. For example, the build command file for the MAIN subsystem might first assign values to macro variables:

```
DB_VERSION = 1.3
UI_VERSION = 2.1
. . .
```

These macro variables are then used to reference elements of the corresponding subsystem:

```
LINK MAIN.O, SYSTEM/DB/DB_VERSION/*.O,
             SYSTEM/UI/UI_VERSION/*.O, etc.
```

Note that these choices of subsystem versions amount to a definition of a configuration thread in the sense discussed in Section 5.5. In this case, however, the items selected are subsystems which themselves consist of a collection of element versions.

6.3 MAKE AND SIMILAR TOOLS

The Make tool for Unix was written by Stuart Feldman at Bell Laboratories during 1975. Since then Make has been widely used and has been very influential. Tools similar to Make have been written for many other operating systems, for example, the VMS tool MMS. More sophisticated tools for defining and building configurations, such as DSEE, are clear descendants of Make. This section will summarise the basic facilities of Make, emphasising the tool's use for defining and building configurations. For a more detailed description of Make see [Feldman 79].

The principal benefit provided by Make is that it builds a configuration using existing versions of derived elements where possible. Suppose that the system held by the simple directory structure of Figure 6.2 is the compiler system described in Section 3.2. Recall that the build command file for this system is

```
CCOMPILE PARSER.C
CCOMPILE CODEGEN.C
ASSEMBLE LEX.ASS
LINK PARSER.O, CODEGEN.O, LEX.O EXE=ACOMP
```

An 'include file' of constant declarations, called CONSTANTS.INC, is included in each of the two C source files, but not in LEX.ASS.

When a new version of PARSER.C is checked into the DEV directory some of the derived elements become out of date and need to be rebuilt—but which? For this very simple system it is clear that the necessary reprocessing is to recompile PARSER.C and then relink ACOMP. For larger systems it is often unclear which derived items need to be rebuilt. Further, how are the required processing commands to be selected from the build command file? The sledgehammer solution is to execute the complete build command file, and so rebuild all derived elements, whenever a source element in a configuration is revised. Make offers a much more efficient alternative to this crude approach.

6.3.1 The Make description file

The Make description file or *Makefile* gives a declarative description of how derived elements depend upon other elements. The Makefile contains a set of *entries,* each of which takes the form

```
target1 target2 ... : ele1 ele2 ele3 ...
    command1
    command2
    command3
    ...
```

The first line of each Makefile entry describes a build dependency: the specified *targets* depend upon the elements listed to the right of the colon. Subsequent lines of the entry are commands which are to be executed if any of the elements become out of date. Usually the targets in a Makefile entry are derived elements which are built by the commands in the entry from the elements listed after the colon. When one of these elements is changed, the derived elements need to be rebuilt.

A Makefile usually contains many entries. The Makefile for the compiler system described at the start of this section is

```
ACOMP : PARSER.O CODEGEN.O LEX.O
   LINK PARSER.O, CODEGEN.O, LEX.O EXE=ACOMP
LEX.O : LEX.ASS
   ASSEMBLE LEX.ASS
PARSER.O : PARSER.C CONSTANTS.INC
   CCOMPILE PARSER.C
CODEGEN.O : CODEGEN.C CONSTANTS.INC
   CCOMPILE CODEGEN.C
```

The four entries in this Makefile constitute a text description of the graph of dependencies illustrated in Figure 3.2. The commands in the Makefile are the processing steps which build the corresponding derived elements.

The Make program takes as input a Makefile and the name of one of the targets in the Makefile. The job of the Make tool is then to produce an up to date version of the target using existing derived elements whenever possible. The basic algorithm which is the core of Make is to update a target by ensuring that all the elements on which it depends exist and are up to date, and then to rebuild the target if it has not been modified since its dependents were modified. Make uses facilities provided by the operating system platform to determine when a file containing an element was last modified.

Make's recursive algorithm amounts to a depth first traversal of the dependency graph; it is most easily understood through an example. Suppose a new revision of CONSTANTS.INC is checked in to the development configuration. To build an up to date version of the executable program, Make is invoked with a target of ACOMP. ACOMP depends on PARSER.O, CODEGEN.O and LEX.O which must therefore be brought up to date. PARSER.O depends on the source elements CONSTANTS.INC, which is out of date, and PARSER.C; PARSER.O must therefore be rebuilt. Similarly CODEGEN.O must be rebuilt. Conversely LEX.O depends only on LEX.ASS which is not out of date, so it does not need to be rebuilt. Having ensured that PARSER.O, CODEGEN.O and LEX.O are up to date, Make determines that ACOMP is older than PARSER.O and CODEGEN.O and therefore relinks ACOMP. Make has performed the following three processing steps:

```
CCOMPILE PARSER.C
CCOMPILE CODEGEN.C
LINK PARSER.O, CODEGEN.O, LEX.O EXE=ACOMP
```

6.3.2 Dummy targets

A Makefile entry may have a *dummy* target, a target which does not correspond to a derived element. Since a dummy target never exists, Make
considers it to be always out of date. The following are the first few lines of a
Makefile for a system containing three executable programs: XPROG, YPROG
and ZPROG.

```
ALLPROGS : XPROG YPROG ZPROG
XPROG : X.O A.O B.O
    LINK X.O, A.O, B.O EXE=XPROG
YPROG : Y.O B.O C.O
. . .
```

The first target in this Makefile is a dummy target; there is no element
called ALLPROGS. Invoking Make with a target of ALLPROGS causes Make
to produce up to date versions of the elements on which ALLPROGS
depends: XPROG, YPROG and ZPROG. This is much more convenient than
invoking Make once for each of these three executable programs.

It is often useful for a Makefile to contain a dummy target which depends
on all derived elements, either directly or indirectly. Invoking Make with
this target ensures that all derived elements are up to date.

6.3.3 Repeated targets

Consider the problem of maintaining a library of object modules S1.O,
S2.O,.... The following Makefile is a simple solution to this problem:

```
LIB : S1.O S2.O ...
    REPLACE LIB S1.O
    REPLACE LIB S2.O
    . . .
```

If any object module is changed LIB is updated by replacing all the object
modules in the library. The problem is that all object modules will be
replaced even if only one is out of date. The following Makefile is a more
economical solution:

```
LIB :: S1.O
    REPLACE LIB S1.O
    LIB :: S2.O
    REPLACE LIB S2.O
    . . .
```

In this Makefile LIB is the target of several entries. The commands executed to update LIB vary in the required way with the object modules which have changed. For example, if only S2.O is changed, only this element will be replaced in the library. The double colon in each Make entry indicates that the target occurs in several entries.

6.3.4 Macros

Make has a macro facility which allows Makefiles to be parametrised. A *macro* is assigned a value either by a line in the Makefile which contains an equals sign or by the command line which invokes Make. A macro is used by preceding its name with a dollar sign; a macro with a name longer than one character must also be enclosed in parentheses when it is used. When Make encounters the use of a macro in a Makefile it substitutes the macro with its value.

The following example uses two macros, OBJECTS and LIBRARY:

```
OBJECTS = X.O, Y.O, Z.O
LIBRARY = LIB1
PROG : $(OBJECTS)
    LINK $(OBJECTS) LIB=$(LIBRARY) EXE=PROG
```

If Make is invoked with a target of PROG, it will build this target using the three object modules and the library LIB1. If the command to invoke Make assigns the value LIB2 to the macro LIBRARY, then this assignment overrides the assignment made within the Makefile and PROG is built using the library LIB2. If the structure of the system changes and an additional object module is needed to link PROG, the only change needed to the Makefile is to the assignment of OBJECTS in the first line.

In general macros are *static*. Make also provides a few *dynamic* macros, the values of which change as the Make program executes. For example, $@ is always the name of the target to be updated and $? is the list of elements which are younger than the target. The next subsection contains an example of the use of a dynamic macro.

6.3.5 Rules

Make maintains a table of *rules* which describe how one type of element is transformed into another. Each rule is defined in terms of the suffices of element names. For example, a rule might state that to transform an element with a suffix .PAS (a '.PAS element') to a .O element the Pascal compiler should be invoked. Make comes with a set of default rules. User supplied rules can be added to this default set to define transformations for element suffices unknown to Make. The default rules can also be overridden.

A rule is itself defined by a Makefile entry of a particular form. The following two entries each define a rule

```
.ASS.O:
    ASSEMBLE $<.ASS
.C.O:
    CCOMPILE $<.C $(COPTIONS)
```

The first rule states that a `.ASS` element is transformed into a `.O` element by the `ASSEMBLE` command. The `$<` is a dynamic macro which takes the value of the prefix of the element used to invoke the rule, in this case the prefix of the `.ASS` element. The second rule is parametrised by the static macro `COPTIONS`; this macro contains the options which will be passed to `CCOMPILE` whenever this rule is used.

Rules allow Makefiles to be considerably shorter and simpler than they would otherwise be. Using the two rules defined above, the Makefile for the compiler system given in Section 6.3.1 can be rewritten as

```
ACOMP : PARSER.O CODEGEN.O LEX.O
    LINK PARSER.O, CODEGEN.O, LEX.O EXE=ACOMP
PARSER.O CODEGEN.O : CONSTANTS.INC
```

6.3.6 Using Make in practice

Makefiles are a more powerful alternative to the build command files described in Section 6.2. The principal benefit of Make is its incremental build facility which dramatically reduces the reprocessing needed to keep an evolving configuration up to date.

Make also provides facilities which address many of the other issues discussed in the context of build command files in Section 6.2.4. For reasons of space some of these facilities have been omitted by the present summary, for example Make's error handling mechanisms.

Like build command files, Makefiles need to be designed carefully; their declarative and highly stylised syntax often leads them to become complicated and opaque. A Makefile must itself be tested, at least as carefully as other source elements. Make can be invoked with an option which causes it to traverse the dependency graph and report the commands that would be executed, without actually executing them; this option is very useful for testing Makefiles.

6.3.7 The limitations of Make

Make must be one of the most successful software tools ever written. It has, however, serious limitations which restrict the benefits of Make for large software projects. The list which follows provides a yardstick for judging more recent tools which define and build configurations.

- *Version selection.* Make does not address the problem of version selection; there is no way to tell Make to use one version of a source element rather than another. Although SCCS is often used with Make, some mechanism not provided by either of these tools is needed to ensure that Make picks up the required version of each source element. The directory structures of Section 6.2 are a very simple example of such a mechanism.

- *Variant derived elements.* Make does not remember details of the tools and options used to build a derived element. Consider the following simple Make entry:

```
X.O : X.PAS
    PASCAL X.PAS $(POPTIONS)
```

  Invoking Make with a target of X.O and the macro POPTIONS set to DEBUG will produce X.O compiled with the DEBUG option. If Make is then invoked, again with a target of X.O but this time with POPTIONS set to OPTIMISE, Make will not rebuild X.O. As far as Make is concerned the existing X.O is good enough—it was built using the most recent version of X.PAS. Unfortunately X.O is not the OPTIMISE variant which is needed.

- *Intermediate derived elements.* Suppose PROG is derived from PROG.O which is itself derived from PROG.PAS. If PROG.O is deleted, perhaps to save disc space in a stable configuration, then Make will rebuild PROG whenever it needs to produce the target PROG, even when PROG.PAS has not changed and the target is in fact up to date.

- *Smart recompilation.* Any change to an element causes Make to rebuild elements which are derived from it. For example, any change to an element of source code prompts Make to recompile. In practice many changes to source code have no effect, or an insignificant effect, upon the derived object module. Adding a comment is a simple example of such a change. A more subtle example is adding a constant declaration to CONSTANTS.INC in the Makefile for the compiler system given in

Section 6.3.1. Unless they too have been modified, PARSER.C and CODEGEN.C (in which CONSTANTS.INC is included) do not need to be recompiled. Make does not realise when a change is insignificant and always rebuilds the target.

- *Deduce dependencies.* Make's in-built and user supplied rules allow some dependencies to be deduced rather than made explicit in the Makefile. The sole basis of Make's deduction of dependencies is the suffix of element names. A more sophisticated tool would examine the content of source elements to deduce more dependencies. For example, the dependency of PARSER.O on CONSTANTS.INC could be deduced by looking for include statements in PARSER.C. Of course this kind of deduction requires the tool to understand the internal structure of elements.

Key Points

- The inputs to defining and building a configuration are source items, the system model, a version selection mechanism and existing derived items.

- The system model is a source item which describes the relationships between the system's source and derived items. In general this description is independent of item versions.

- The system model must be designed at least as carefully as other source items. It should parametrise and automate the build process, and should manage errors during the build.

- Simple operating system facilities may be used to define and build configurations: directories to hold configurations and command files to serve as system models.

- The Make tool builds a configuration using existing derived elements where possible. Make's system model (Makefile) is a compact and declarative description of the system's build dependencies.

- Make has limitations which make it difficult to use for large systems. Make's most serious limitation is its ignorance of element versions.

7

DSEE, A SECOND GENERATION CM ENVIRONMENT

The DSEE CM environment is a major advance upon earlier tools for defining and building configurations, not least in the way it addresses several of Make's limitations. DSEE, which stands for the Domain Software Engineering Environment and is traditionally pronounced 'dizzy', runs on HP Apollo workstations. The designers of DSEE were influenced by experimental environments developed at Xerox PARC (see, for example, [Lampson 83]). This chapter describes the most important features of this important tool.

DSEE has four components. The History Manager stores versions of source elements in a library. The principles of the History Manager are similar to tools like SCCS and RCS and are not described here in detail. The component concerned with defining and building configurations is called the Configuration Manager; it is this aspect of DSEE which is described in some detail in this chapter. The other two components of DSEE, the Task Manager and Monitor Manager, provide mechanisms for controlling the process of changing software; this aspect of CM will be discussed in later chapters in the context of change control.

Defining and building a configuration using DSEE is based on three concepts:

- The *system model* is DSEE's analogue of a Makefile. It identifies the source elements, tools (which DSEE calls translators) and procedures used to build derived elements. It does not identify versions of elements.

- The *configuration thread* is a set of rules from which DSEE deduces the versions of elements and tools which are to be used to build derived elements. The thread also specifies the options which are to be passed to tools.

- The *derived element pool* is a cache of derived elements. When a derived element is built it is added to the pool which may contain several versions of each derived element. Each element in the pool is tagged with a *bound configuration thread (BCT)* which lists the versions of all source elements used to build the derived element, as well as all tool versions and options. Developers working on different configurations are able to share derived elements by using the same pool.

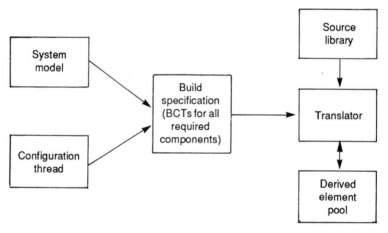

Figure 7.1   Building with DSEE

Figure 7.1 shows the relationship between these concepts. When DSEE is instructed to build a derived element it combines the system model and configuration thread to produce a BCT for the required derived element. DSEE then searches the derived element pool for existing derived elements which can be reused to build the required element. Like Make, DSEE traverses the dependency graph implied by the system model, building the derived elements it needs. Make reuses a derived element providing the elements used to build it have not subsequently changed; DSEE reuses a derived element if its BCT matches the required BCT. An important benefit of DSEE's approach is that it allows configurations to share derived elements whenever possible.

As derived elements are built they are added to the derived element pool. When elements fall into disuse they are purged from the pool. DSEE can be instructed to keep a certain number of versions of a derived element and to keep a derived element for a minimum period. When these limits are exceeded DSEE deletes the derived element which has been used least recently. Of course, derived elements which DSEE has purged can always be rebuilt from their sources.

7.1 THE SYSTEM MODEL

The system model describes the relationships between the components of a system. In DSEE terminology, a component is either an independently *buildable component* of the system or a *leaf component*. A leaf component, i.e. one that is not derived from other components, is either a *source element* or a *translator* such as a compiler.

7.1.1 The block structure

The system model of a large system can become very complex. DSEE provides a way of structuring the system model as a hierarchy of nested blocks. In this respect, the difference between a Makefile and a DSEE system model is analogous to the difference between FORTRAN and a block structured language like Pascal. Each block in the system model corresponds to a buildable component of the system. There are three main types of blocks:

- A single *model block* encompasses the entire system and defines properties of the system as a whole.

- An *element block* represents a buildable component which corresponds to a source element. The component may also depend upon other elements, but the source element which names the block is the *primary dependency* of the component.

- An *aggregate block* has no primary source dependency but comprises subordinate elements and aggregate blocks. Aggregate blocks decompose the system into a hierarchy of design items as discussed in Chapter 3.

Figure 7.2 is an incomplete system module for the ACOMP compiler. Each of the enclosed regions of the figure is a block: ACOMP is the model block which contains the entire system; FRONT_END and BACK_END are aggregate blocks; LEX.ASS, PARSER.C and CODEGEN.C are element blocks.

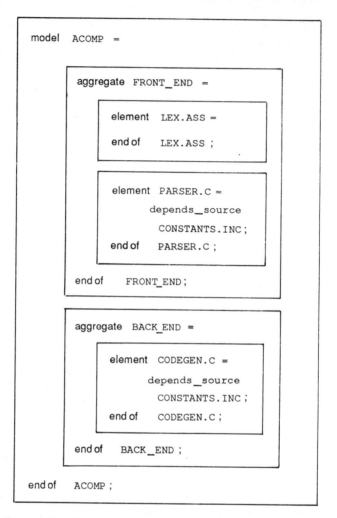

Figure 7.2   The block structure of a system model for ACOMP

7.1.2 Dependency declarations

The declarations inside each block identify other components on which the component depends and describe the translation rule which builds the component. There are three types of dependency, one for each type of component:

- *Depends_source* declarations identify the source elements which the component depends upon directly. An element block is implicitly dependent upon its primary source. Other source dependencies are usually the include files required by the component's primary source. In Figure 7.2 the component PARSER.C is implicitly dependent upon the source element of the same name; it also depends upon CONSTANTS.INC.

- *Depends_tool* declarations identify the tools used to build the component. It is not essential to declare tools as dependencies; if a tool dependency is declared then the version of the tool is recorded in the component's BCT.

- *Depends_result* declarations identify other components, often sub-components of the current component, the derived elements of which are needed to build the component.

7.1.3 Translation rules

A *translation rule* is a series of commands which build the derived elements of the component. Not all blocks have a translation rule, for example, an aggregate block which defines a group of logically related components does not have a translation rule.

Translation rules are parametrised in terms of the sources and results of the translation; this allows the same rule to be used for many components. Keywords starting with the % character are special symbols which take particular values when the translation rule is used: %source is the name of the component's primary source dependency; %result_of denotes the derived elements produced by the components specified as an argument to the symbol; %result is the name of the derived element produced by the translation; %done simply denotes the end of the translation rule.

The following complete system model for the ACOMP system illustrates the use of translation rules and dependency declarations.

```
model ACOMP =
    translate
       LINK %result_of(*) EXE=%result
    %done;
    depends_result
       aggregate FRONT_END =
            element LEX.ASS =
                translate
                    ASSEMBLE %source %result
                %done;
            end of LEX.ASS;
```

```
          element PARSER.C =
              depends_source CONSTANTS.INC;
              translate
                  CCOMPILE %source %result
              %done;
          end of PARSER.C;
      end of FRONT_END;
      aggregate BACK_END =
          element CODEGEN.C =
              depends_source CONSTANTS.INC;
              translate
                  CCOMPILE %source %result
              %done;
          end of CODEGEN.C;
      end of BACK_END;
  end of ACOMP;
```

7.1.4 Defaults

Normally a declaration applies only to the block in which it appears. A *default declaration* applies to all subblocks of the block containing the default. Defaults can be used for translation rules (where they serve as DSEE's analogue of the Make rules described in Section 6.3.5) and also for dependencies. The following default could be used in the ACOMP model block to declare that all subblocks having a name with suffix of .C are to be compiled using CCOMPILE and have a source dependency on CONSTANTS.INC.

```
default for *.C =
    translate
      CCOMPILE %source %result
    %done;
    depends_source CONSTANTS.INC;
end of *.C;
```

7.1.5 Dependencies across the block hierarchy

Often a component depends upon components which are not subcomponents. For example, a block in the system model which corresponds to a subsystem might link an executable program using object modules, some of which are built by a different subsystem. In this case the depends_result declaration needs to refer to a component which is not a subcomponent.

A dependency declaration can only refer to blocks which are visible from the dependent component. The visibility of a block in the system model is defined by a scoping rule similar to that of a block structured language: a block is visible from anywhere within its parent block, including subblocks of the parent block. This rule also corresponds to the rule for item visibility described in Section 3.6. The system model must be structured so that components are visible from other components which depend upon their results.

7.1.6 Generating the system model

A DSEE tool called Make_model can be used to generate automatically a first-cut system model from a collection of source elements. Make_model scans source elements looking for include directives which imply source dependencies in the system model. The partial model generated by Make_model is then refined and completed manually. Unfortunately, there is no way of ensuring that the accuracy of the source dependencies is preserved as further include directives are added to the source elements and the model is changed.

7.2 BUILDING A COMPONENT

The first step in building a DSEE component is to select the required system model. For a small system this is simply a matter of directing DSEE to the source element which contains the system model. For a large system the system model may consist of several DSEE elements; versions of these elements are selected using a *model thread*. A model thread is similar to a configuration thread, except that it applies to the system model rather than the entire system. The technique of storing all variants within a single element is particularly powerful for variant system models. The DSEE system model language incorporates a preprocessor which is similar to the C preprocessor described in Section 4.4.3. When the system model is selected it is preprocessed to give a model which builds the required variant of the system.

The next step in building a component is to specify a *configuration thread*. The thread instructs DSEE which versions of source elements are to be used and which options are to be passed to translators. Section 7.4 describes configuration threads in detail.

Once the thread has been specified, DSEE can be instructed to build a component of the system model. To build a component DSEE must also build all its subcomponents. For example, using the system model for the ACOMP system in Section 7.1.3, if DSEE is instructed to build FRONT_END it must build both LEX.ASS and PARSER.C. DSEE will not rebuild a component if a suitable version is already in the derived element pool. The following example illustrates a build using DSEE (the system model and configuration thread have already been specified), where the first line is a DSEE build command and subsequent lines are messages issued by DSEE:

```
DSEE>build LEX.ASS
Building LEX.ASS
Build LEX.ASS!30-March-1991.15:16:05
No errors, no warnings, ASSEMBLER version 1.2
```

When a component is built it is added to the derived element pool where it is identified by its full build name. The *full build name* comprises the name of the component, an exclamation point and the build version which is defined by the date and time of the build. The full build name of the component built by the build command above is

```
LEX.ASS!30-March-1991.15:16:05
```

There is a DSEE command which lists all the builds of a component that are currently in the derived element pool. Another command displays the BCT of a build, i.e. the translation rules and element versions used in the build; this command also displays the system model used to build the component and the build command line.

All the source elements used in a build can be tagged with a name. For example, the DSEE command

```
name version ACOMP! V1.0
```

gives the name V1.0 to all the source elements used in the most recent build of the ACOMP compiler. The absence of a date and time after the exclamation point in a full build name is a shorthand for the most recent build of the component.

Naming a DSEE element is similar to including an element in a CMS class as described in Section 5.5.2. Element versions with the same name are logically connected and can be referred to collectively. For example, the elements which share the name V1.0 might constitute the source elements for version 1.0 of the ACOMP compiler.

7.3 EXPORTING DERIVED ELEMENTS FROM THE POOL

Any derived element in the pool can be copied out of the pool. DSEE's caching algorithm means that a derived element in the pool may be purged if it has not been recently used. The algorithm can be overridden by instructing DSEE that particular derived elements must not be purged.

Another mechanism for exporting derived elements from the pool is to create a *release*. The DSEE release command copies derived elements and their BCTs to a release directory. For example, the DSEE command

```
create release /ACOMP_RLS -from ACOMP!
```

creates a release directory called /ACOMP_RLS and copies into it all derived elements and BCTs of the most recent build of the ACOMP compiler. Options and parameters of the create release command, which are not used in this example, can be used to instruct DSEE to copy only a subset of the derived elements and BCTs to the release directory.

Derived elements in a release directory can be accessed independently of DSEE and are never purged as they might be from the pool. A release directory can be passed to any DSEE command in the place of a full build name: instead of looking for derived elements and BCTs in the derived element pool, DSEE looks in the release directory.

7.4 THE CONFIGURATION THREAD

The system model describes the structure of the system. It does not specify which versions and options are to be used for a particular build; this information is provided by the configuration thread.

The configuration thread is a set of rules written in the configuration thread language. Each rule occupies a single line of the thread and contains either one or both of:

- A *version rule*, which describes the versions of source elements which are to be used.

- An *option rule*, which describes the options to be used by a translator.

The simplest configuration thread, the default thread, is simply

```
[]
```

This rule states that the most recent version of all source elements is to be used. Another thread which is often used is

```
-reserved
[]
```

The first rule states that if an element is checked out, or in DSEE termi-nology reserved, from the DSEE library then the reserved version in the developer's working directory should be used. The rules in a thread are in priority order so that for elements which are not reserved the most recent version is used.

Version and option rules can be preceded by a *rule qualifier* which restricts the applicability of the rules which follow to particular components of the model. A rule qualifier starts with -for or -under; if there is no rule qualifier then the rules which follow apply to all components of the model. The following rule comprises a rule qualifier and an option rule (but no version rule).

```
-for *.C -use_options DEBUG
```

The rule qualifier states that the rule which follows only applies to components of the system model with a suffix of .C. The option rule states that translators are to be used with the DEBUG option.

7.4.1 Version rules

A version rule can identify a version explicitly. The following rule specifies that version 5 of CONSTANTS.INC be used.

```
-for CONSTANTS.INC [5]
```

It is quite unusual for a rule to identify a source element version explicitly in this way.

Section 7.2 noted that a version of one or more source elements can be given a symbolic name. For example, one version for each of a set of source elements could be deemed fit for integration testing and assigned the version name TEST. The following rule selects the source elements for subcomponents of the FRONT_END component which have a version name of TEST:

```
-under FRONT_END [TEST]
```

where -under qualifies the rule to apply to all subcomponents of the aggregate FRONT_END. The -under rule qualifier allows different versions of the same element to be used in different components of the model; this is a powerful but dangerous DSEE facility that must be used very carefully!

Version rules can also be used to select a variant line of descent for source elements. The following rule selects the most recent version on the FIX branch for all elements:

```
.../FIX -when_exists
```

where -when_exists means that if an element does not have a branch called FIX then the rule is ignored. The rule will also be ignored if the variant line of descent has been merged with the main line of descent, as in Figure 5.2. The case study in Section 7.8 provides further examples of these version rules.

7.4.2 Option rules

A translation rule may be hardwired in the system model; for example, the rule

```
CCOMPILE %source %result DEBUG
```

means that CCOMPILE is always used with the DEBUG option. Alternatively, the system model may leave the choice of certain options to the configuration thread. For example, the translation rule

```
CCOMPILE %source %result %option(DEBUG)
```

allows an option rule in the configuration thread to determine whether or not CCOMPILE is invoked with the DEBUG option. The following thread illustrates a typical use of option rules:

```
-reserved -use_options DEBUG
/FIX -when_exists -use_options DEBUG
[]
```

This thread uses the DEBUG option for all reserved elements or for elements for which there is a variant called FIX, but not for other elements.

7.4.3 Build based rules

A rule can instruct DSEE to use the same versions or the same rules as were used in a previous build. A build can be identified by its date and time. More usually, and more reliably, build based rules refer to release directories as in

```
-under FRONT_END ACOMP!/V1.0 -versions -options
```

This rule states that for subcomponents of the aggregate FRONT_END, the same versions and options are to be used as were used in the build of ACOMP in the release directory /V1.0.

7.5 THE RESERVED POOL

Recall that a configuration thread may specify the reserved version of a source element. Derived elements built from reserved elements are usually only of interest to the developer who has the element reserved. Furthermore, working revisions made to a reserved element are uncontrolled: they do not correspond to identifiable versions of the element and typically overwrite the previous working revision.

For these reasons DSEE does not store derived elements which are built from reserved elements in the central, shared, derived element pool. Instead, each DSEE user has a *reserved pool* which holds those derived elements which depend on reserved source elements.

When a reserved element is checked in to the DSEE library, derived elements may be promoted from the reserved pool to the central derived element pool. A derived element is promoted if all the reserved elements which it depends upon have been checked in, and none of these elements has been changed since the derived element was built.

7.6 AVOIDING UNNECESSARY REBUILDS

The simplest algorithm for reusing derived elements from the pool is to reuse an element if its BCT is precisely as required. In practice this requirement is sometimes too stringent and leads to unnecessary processing. DSEE provides the three mechanisms described in this section which allow a derived element to be reused even though its BCT is not an exact match.

7.6.1 Non-critical options

Suppose that a translation rule in the system model reads

```
CCOMPILE %source %result %options(DEBUG)
```

and that a rule in the configuration thread requests

```
-for PARSER.C -use_options DEBUG
```

When DSEE is instructed to build PARSER.C for the first time it will invoke CCOMPILE with the DEBUG option. Once PARSER.C has been debugged the thread rule for PARSER.C will be changed to request that the DEBUG option is not used:

```
-for PARSER.C -use_options
```

If DSEE is then instructed to rebuild PARSER.C it reuses the derived element in the pool, even though the element was compiled with the DEBUG option. The reason is that the translation rule in the system model implies that the DEBUG option is non-critical, i.e. the option is not a crucial property of the derived element.

There are two ways of ensuring that a derived element is built with exactly the options specified by the system model and the configuration thread. The first is to designate the option as critical in the system model. If the translation rule is changed to

```
CCOMPILE %source %result %critical_options(DEBUG)
```

then DSEE will build the component with precisely the option requested by the thread. The second is for the thread to demand that a component is built with exactly the requested options, for example

```
-for PARSER.C -use_options -exact
```

7.6.2 Non-critical dependencies

The system model describes how a component depends upon source elements, tools and the derived elements of other components. Any dependency can be designated non-critical; this means that the component will not be rebuilt merely to use the requested versions of the dependency. Instead a derived element from the pool will be used providing its BCT matches the desired BCT for the critical dependencies. This laxity can be overridden by an option of the BUILD command.

A dependency is designated as non-critical if there is usually no need to rebuild the component just because the dependency has changed. For example, dependencies on an include file might be designated non-critical. When a declaration is added to the include file, components which do not use the declaration do not need to be rebuilt; conversely, components which do use the declaration will be rebuilt anyway because the dependent element in which the element is included will have changed.

7.6.3 Equivalences

Suppose that the only difference between versions 4 and 5 of LEX.ASS is that the later revision contains documentation as comments. These two versions can be declared to be equivalent, thereby ensuring that components built with version 4 are not rebuilt merely because of their dependency on LEX.ASS. An equivalence can be declared which is effective either for the duration of the current build or until the equivalent derived elements are removed from the pool.

This and the earlier two mechanisms provide ways of telling DSEE not to worry about certain options, dependencies and versions when building components. This can be very useful when building experimental versions. When a component is to be issued to a customer it is good and safe practice to spurn these shortcuts and build the component cleanly and precisely.

7.7 PARALLEL BUILDING

Workstations running DSEE are usually connected in a network. Typically each DSEE user has a workstation in the network. The network may contain additional server nodes such as file servers and compute servers. Files are shared between nodes of the network: one node can access a file on another as if the file were on the same node.

Early versions of DSEE built components in series using the CPU of the node which requested the build. Recent versions of DSEE build components in parallel using many CPUs throughout the network. Building in parallel produces exactly the same results as serial building, but does so more quickly.

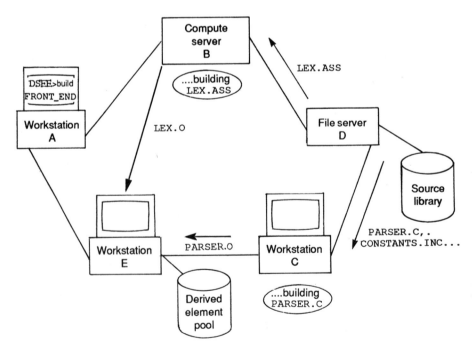

Figure 7.3   Building ACOMP in parallel using DSEE

Figure 7.3 illustrates the parallel build facility. A user on workstation A instructs DSEE to build component FRONT_END of the ACOMP system described in Section 7.1.3. DSEE determines that LEX.ASS and PARSER.C need to be built and that these components are independent of each other and can therefore be built in parallel. DSEE then selects nodes B and C to build the subcomponents in parallel; each of these nodes reads the source elements it needs from the library on node D and writes derived elements to the pool on node E.

The system model defines a partial order for building components. This partial order is the only constraint on the sequence in which the components are built. If processing steps must be performed in a stricter order than that implied by the dependencies, then they must be enclosed in a single translation rule of the system model. Cases of this kind arise when a derived element is built by more than one processing step. (Make deals with such cases by guaranteeing to scan the dependency tree defined by the Makefile in a particular order, namely depth first. Unfortunately this guarantee precludes any possibility of parallel processing.)

Building a system in parallel poses several interesting problems including:

- *Node selection.* How is DSEE to select a node on which to build a component? The principal objective is to select the node which will build the component most quickly, but there are other factors such as to what extent it is acceptable to degrade the performance of the chosen node.

- *User interface.* How are the results of building components in parallel to be presented to the user? There are two considerations: the user must be kept informed of the process of the build but the parallel processing should not unduly complicate the user interface.

For details of DSEE's solutions to these and other problems see [Leblang 87] and [Leblang 88].

7.8 CASE STUDY: USING DSEE TO MAINTAIN AND DEVELOP A SOFTWARE PRODUCT

This case study is presented with two objectives. Firstly, to show how the DSEE facilities described in this chapter may be used in practice. Secondly, to illustrate a method of version management which is suitable for developing a new version of a software product while at the same time maintaining the version which has been issued to users. Although DSEE supports this method very effectively, similar approaches are feasible using less sophisticated tools, for example MMS and CMS with CMS classes taking the place of DSEE names.

The case study does not address all the concerns of CM, but concentrates on those that demonstrate the practical use of DSEE. There is no discussion here of how changes to elements are proposed, reviewed, tested and approved. Further, the design item hierarchy does not contain items between the level of elements and the complete system. Although DSEE can be used to address these CM concerns, DSEE's greatest strengths lie in the areas covered in the case study.

7.8.1 The problem

Version 1.0 of the ACOMP compiler has been developed, tested and released to several users. The engineers who wrote the compiler are now responsible for developing version 2.0 to include features which have been added to the ACOMP language. Version 2.0 is to be developed in a series of internal versions: 1.1, 1.2, etc. These internal versions will not be issued to users but will be tested within the supplier organisation. Serious faults must be fixed in internal versions so that testing can continue. The engineers must also support version 1.0 of the compiler: faults must be fixed and the fixes must be released to users. CM requirements of this kind are extremely common during the development and maintenance of a software product.

7.8.2 Identifying versions of the ACOMP compiler

The concurrent support and development of the ACOMP compiler demands many versions of the system: internal versions, versions issued to users and fault fix versions. Figure 7.4 shows how versions of the compiler are identified. Fault fix versions of the ACOMP compiler have suffices of A, B, C, etc. The V which precedes each version identifier is simply to allow the identifier to serve as the name of a DSEE release.

At any time fault fixes are only needed to the most recent internal version of the compiler: version V1.2 becomes obsolete as soon as version V1.3 is built. Bug fixes are needed to version V1.0 until version V2.0 is available; at that time the supplier organisation unilaterally stops supporting version V1.0 and requires users to upgrade to V2.0!

When a version of the ACOMP compiler is built, a DSEE release is created in a subdirectory of /RELEASES. For example, the first version of the compiler is held as !/RELEASES/V1.0. Released builds make the ACOMP compiler available for distribution and testing and allow these versions to be referenced from DSEE during subsequent development and maintenance work.

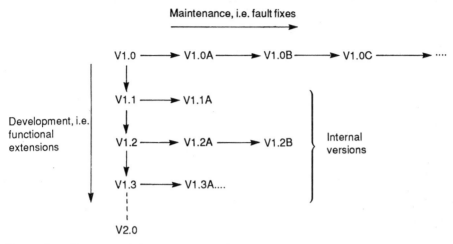

Figure 7.4   Versions of the ACOMP compiler

7.8.3 Identifying element versions

The version of each source element used in each release is given the name of the version of the ACOMP compiler to which it belongs. Thus if version 3 of CODEGEN.C is used in version V1.2A of the compiler then it is given the name V1.2A.

Elements are named as soon as the version of the compiler in which they are used is built and released. For example, when version V1.2A is released all its source elements are named by the DSEE command:

```
name version ACOMP!/RELEASES/V1.2A V1.2A
```

The name of an element version should not be confused with its DSEE version number. The version number of LEX.ASS and PARSER.C in V1.2 may be 7 and 27 respectively, although both will have a version name of V1.2. The version number of CODEGEN.C[V1.1] might be the same as that of CODEGEN.C[V1.1A] or, if many changes were made to that element for the fault fix version, will be much greater. Note that DSEE allows one element version to have more than one name.

Version names tie together all related element versions with one logical mnemonic name. In this case study it is the version name of an element, not its number, which is significant.

7.8.4 Using branches for fault fixes

For each element of the ACOMP compiler, the main line of descent is used for development work and branch lines of descent are used for fault fixes. Every fault fix branch originates from the element version used in the corresponding version of the compiler; the name of each branch is the name of the compiler version followed by _FIX. For example, the branch containing fault fixes to LEX.ASS, for version V1.1 of the compiler originates from LEX.ASS[V1.1] and is called V1.1_FIX.

Recall from Section 4.3.1 the maxim that temporary variants should be merged sooner rather than later. Consistent with this maxim, each internal version of the ACOMP compiler includes all fault fixes so far made to version V1.0. Further, a fix to an internal version of the ACOMP compiler is immediately included in the main line of descent if no development changes have been made to the element since the branch was started. The DSEE automated merge tool described in Subsection 4.4.2 is used to add fault fixes to each element's main line of descent.

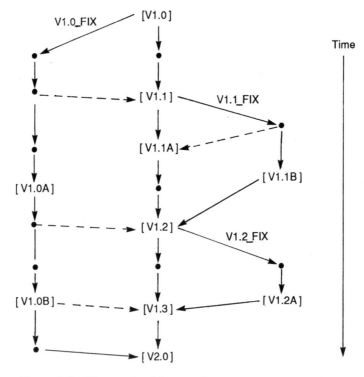

Figure 7.5   The version history of LEX.ASS

Figure 7.5 depicts the evolution of one element of the ACOMP compiler. Each dot on the figure denotes an unnamed version of LEX.ASS. Bug fix branches of descent are shown to either side of the main line of descent.

The branch V1.0_FIX holds fault fixes to version 1.0. The dashed lines on Figure 7.5 which leave this branch indicate that whenever an internal version of the ACOMP compiler is built, fault fixes are merged into the main line of descent. Note that the V1.0_FIX branch continues after merges for internal versions; the branch is only closed off when version V2.0 of the compiler is built and version V1.0 is no longer supported.

The branches V1.1_FIX and V1.2_FIX hold fixes to internal versions. These branches are merged with the main line of descent when the next internal version is built. Note that a fault fix to LEX.ASS for version V1.1 is needed before any development work has been done on LEX.ASS; this fix is therefore immediately included in the main line of descent. On the other hand, by the time the first fault is fixed in LEX.ASS[V1.2] development changes have already been made to the element.

7.8.5 Defining and building fault fix configurations

The following configuration thread is used to build fault fix versions of V1.0 of the ACOMP compiler:

```
.../V1.0_FIX -when_exists
ACOMP!/RELEASES/V1.0 -versions -options -exact
```

The first thread rule instructs DSEE that if an element has a branch called V1.0_FIX, then the most recent element on that branch should be used. This rule ensures that all fixes to version V1.0 are included in the build. For elements not selected by the first rule, the versions used in release V1.0 are to be used, and these elements are to be compiled and linked using exactly the options used when V1.0 was built.

An alternative way of defining fault fix versions of V1.0 would be to use the thread

```
.../V1.0_FIX -when_exists
[V1.0]
```

This thread selects the same element versions as the first, but does not ensure that the same options are used as were used when V1.0 was built.

An engineer fixing a fault in his or her working directory tests fixes before replacing elements in the DSEE library by prefacing either of the above threads with the rule

```
-reserved -use_options -debug
```

Key Points

- DSEE is a second generation CM tool for defining and building configurations; it overcomes many of the limitations of tools like SCCS and Make.

- DSEE stores derived elements in a pool which is shared by all DSEE users. Each derived element is tagged with its derivation. Elements from the pool are used to build configurations whenever possible.

- A DSEE configuration thread is a set of rules which defines the element versions, tools and tool options that are used to build a configuration.

- DSEE allows tool options and item dependencies to be designated non-critical, i.e. insignificant for the purpose of building a particular configuration. Versions of source elements can also be designated as equivalent.

- DSEE may use several nodes in a network of workstations to build derived elements in parallel. The distribution of the software library and of build processing is largely transparent to the DSEE user.

8

THE CM REQUIREMENTS OF ADA AND THE RATIONAL ENVIRONMENT

This chapter concentrates on the CM requirements of Ada. The first section describes the characteristics of Ada which affect CM; the second section outlines the Rational Environment's approach to these issues. Although some of the discussion is specific to Ada, most of the CM principles which Ada highlights are applicable to all types of item—not just Ada source code.

8.1 ADA: A CHALLENGE AND AN OPPORTUNITY

This section reviews Ada from a CM perspective. It concentrates on the features which make Ada suitable for developing large systems that comprise many millions of lines of code. There is no discussion here of Ada syntax or of its support for 'programming in the small'. The 'programming in the large' features of Ada which are significant for CM are:

- *Information hiding.* Ada makes a clear distinction between the specification (or interface) of Ada code and the body of the code. The specification describes everything which users of the code need to know and may depend upon; the body is the implementation of the interface as executable Ada code.

- *Separation of specification and body.* A specification and body may be managed as separate Ada compilation units and therefore, in CM terms, as distinct elements. Each unit can be compiled separately. This

P

```
package P is
  function PRIME ( N : in INTEGER ) return BOOLEAN is
  -- Return TRUE if N is prime
    .
    .
    .
end P;
```

S

```
with P;

procedure S ( N: in out  INTEGER ) is
-- Change N to be the next prime number
begin
  for N in N... INTEGER'LAST loop
    exit when P.PRIME ( N );
  end loop;
end S;
```

WITH

ELABORATES

P_body

```
package body P is
  function PRIME  ( N : in INTEGER ) return BOOLEAN is
    I = INTEGER;
  begin
    for I  in 2 ...N/2  loop
      if ( N/I )*I =N then
        return FALSE ;
      endif;
    end loop;
    return TRUE;
  end PRIME;
    .
    .
    .
end P;
```

flexibility enables both top-down and bottom-up approaches to software development. In a top-down approach high level specifications are developed, which are then implemented as bodies; in a bottom-up approach fully elaborated Ada code is written which then serves as a building block in assembling a complete system. Each of these approaches must be coordinated by CM.

• *Checking between separately compiled units.* An Ada compilation system checks that the unit it is compiling is consistent with all the other units on which it depends. This check is often called *semantic consistency*. It distinguishes Ada from most other compilation systems. FORTRAN subroutines can be compiled separately but the compiler does not check, for example, that one subroutine calls another with the correct arguments; Pascal compilers do perform such checks, but only within a single file submitted to the compiler.

These are powerful facilities for developing large software systems which have important implications on how configurations of Ada programs are defined and built. The discussion which follows describes CM principles, not Ada details. [Booch 87] is a good introduction to Ada whereas [ANSI 83] is the definitive description of the language.

8.1.1 Dependencies between Ada units

An Ada system is divided into a set of elements each of which is submitted as a whole to the Ada compiler. An element is usually a file held by the operating system. Each element contains one or more Ada *units*. A unit is either the specification or the body of an Ada structuring construct such as a package or a subprogram. How many Ada units to include in one element is determined by the considerations described in Section 3.1, but is best kept small.

Ada units may depend upon each other in one of two ways. A *with* dependency arises when one unit uses resources, such as procedures and data definitions, which are provided by another unit. The principle of information hiding dictates that the referenced unit is a specification. An *elaboration* dependency is the dependency between a specification and the body which implements the specification. Neither type of dependency is a build dependency; sadly, unless you happen to earn your living as a programmer, the body of a package is not derived by automatic processing of its specification.

Figure 8.1 shows these dependencies between three elements of Ada code: the combined specification and body of a procedure S and the separate

Figure 8.1   Three elements of Ada code and their dependencies specification and body of a package P which is used by S. The Ada code in the boxes is merely to illustrate how these dependencies might arise.

8.1.2 The Ada program library

An Ada program library contains a description of a consistent set of Ada units which is maintained by the compiler. When an Ada unit is compiled its description is added to the library; if the unit has been compiled before, the old description is overwritten.

It is the program library which allows the Ada compiler to check the semantic consistency of separately compiled units. The compiler reads from the library information about units on which the new unit depends. If the new unit is not consistent with the units it depends upon, the compilation fails and the library is not updated. On the other hand, units which depend upon the new unit are deleted from the library: their consistency with the new unit can no longer be guaranteed and they need to be recompiled. For the example of Figure 8.1, when a new version of P_body is compiled the compiler checks that the body is a valid elaboration of the specification P. When the specification P is recompiled the library units P_body and S are deleted from the library; these units depend on P and must be recompiled against the new specification of P.

The structure of an Ada program library varies between Ada environments. The Rational Environment represents each library unit as a DIANA tree [Goos 83]. A DIANA tree is the product of the semantic analysis phase of an Ada compilation. This representation provides the compiler with the information it needs to check the consistency of dependent units. It is then also the basis for other tools of an Ada compilation system, for example a static analyser which detects anomalies in source code and a pretty printer which lays out code in a standard and readable way. As is illustrated in Figure 8.2, the program library is the heart of an Ada compilation system.

8.1.3 Compilation order

An important consequence of Ada's approach to semantic integrity is that it restricts the order in which units are compiled. The basic rule is that a unit must be compiled before all other units which depend upon it. Of the three units of Figure 8.1, P must be compiled before either P_body or S.

For a large Ada system, compiling units in the correct order calls for delicate judgement. It is possible to maintain a command file or a Makefile which compiles, in an appropriate order, both a specified unit and all other units that depend upon it. Unfortunately Makefiles become hard to write and maintain when, as with Ada, there are many dependencies and the order of compilation is significant.

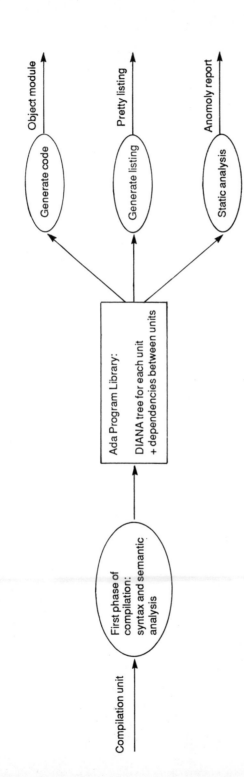

Figure 8.2 An Ada compilation system

A better approach is for a CM tool to determine compilation requirements automatically from the dependencies defined by the Ada source. Some Ada environments include tools which generate Makefiles. Other environments use the dependencies recorded in the program to take complete control of the compilation process. Note that with this approach the software developer is not required to maintain a separate system model; instead, the system model is derived from the Ada source code.

8.1.4 Smart recompilation

In principle, changing an Ada specification renders obsolete all library units which have been compiled against the old specification. Each unit which is dependent upon the specification must be recompiled, even though the unit might not need to be revised. In practice, many of these recompilations are unnecessary. There are two important cases in which a unit does not need to be recompiled, even though it is dependent on an element which has been revised:

- *Upward compatible changes.* An upward compatible revision to a specification is one which extends the previous specification, for example adding a procedure to an Ada package. Other units are not affected by an upward compatible revision.

- *Changes which do not affect a dependent unit.* Suppose an Ada package is revised by changing the value of a constant which is defined by the package specification. A unit which uses the revised package must be recompiled if and only if it makes use of the constant.

A smart approach to recompilation is one which performs no more recompilations than are strictly necessary. Smart recompilation is not specific to Ada. The discussion of non-critical dependencies between DSEE elements in Section 7.6 is concerned with precisely this issue. Smart compilation is, however, particularly important for Ada. A program written in Ada has many more explicit dependencies than the same program written in, for example, C; of course the dependencies are there in the C program, but they are implicit and the C compiler does not recognise them. For a detailed analysis of smart recompilation see [Tichy 86].

8.1.5 Managing the program library

In CM terms, an Ada program library is a derived element. It must be managed according to the principles of version management and identification established in Chapters 4 and 5. A CM environment for Ada must ensure that:

- *The program library exists as a set of identified versions.* Not every compilation of an Ada unit should create a new version of the library. After unit P of Figure 8.1 is compiled, the dependent library units P_body and S are potentially obsolete. This incomplete version of the library is probably not worth preserving as a version—unless, perhaps, the new specification of P requires significant development work to dependent units rather than merely recompilation. The software developer must decide when a program library should be preserved as a version, and the CM environment must implement that decision.

- *The derivation of each version of the library is recorded.* Each version of the program library must be uniquely identified. The derivation of the library must also be recorded, preferably within the program library itself. Many Ada environments store the version identification of the source text for each library unit.

- *Any version of the library can be used for further work.* A developer may wish to use old versions of the program library, for example, as a basis for a fault fix version of issued software. An Ada CM environment must make available all versions of the program library, not just the most recent working version.

8.1.6 Subsystem libraries

A large Ada project will wish to develop many subsystems in parallel. Each subsystem will have its own program library with its own change history. At some stage these subsystems will be integrated and dependencies between different subsystems resolved.

A crude solution to this problem is to recompile all source units into a single program library when the subsystems are integrated. A much better solution is to allow one subsystem to refer to library units in another subsystem. A CM environment for Ada must enable both the parallel evolution of program libraries and the integration of these libraries without wholesale recompilation.

8.2 CM IN THE RATIONAL ENVIRONMENT

The Rational Environment is a software engineering environment for developing large systems using Ada. Many of the environment's capabilities are specific to elements which are Ada units; however, elements can also be documents or source code written in a language other than Ada. The environment runs on its own purpose designed hardware platform. The Rational Environment was developed in the early 1980s and has been in commercial use since 1985.

This section concentrates on one key aspect of the Rational Environment: its approach to CM. Other innovative aspects of the environment, such as those which provide interactive debugging and static analysis of Ada programs, will not be described. Rational's approach to CM is interesting both for the way it solves the issues specific to Ada, which were raised in the previous section, and for its approach to the general problem of defining and building configurations.

8.2.1 Subsystems and views

The design item hierarchy for a software system developed using the Rational Environment has two levels. The system is divided into subsystems each of which comprises elements. Guidelines for how to partition a system into subsystems were discussed in Chapter 3. Each subsystem should be a logical component of the system with a well-defined interface with other subsystems. A typical subsystem in the Rational Environment contains between five and twenty-five thousand lines of Ada and is developed by up to five engineers.

Subsystems contain versions of elements in a similar way to, for example, SCCS and DSEE. The Rational Environment also manages versions of subsystems which are called *views*; a view contains one version of each element in the subsystem. A view corresponds to a CMS class or a DSEE thread. Element versions which are part of a view are held by the Rational Environment in their entirety, other elements are stored as deltas.

There are two types of view: *working views* and *release views*. A working view is mutable; it provides a work area for development work. To revise an element a developer checks the element out to a working view where it can be modified. The other element versions in the working view provide the context for these modifications. When the modifications are complete the developer checks in the element. This creates a new revision of the element and updates the working view so that it contains this new revision. A release view, on the other hand, iş a snapshot of a working view; once a release view has been defined it cannot be changed. Figure 8.3 shows a series of release views which are snapshots of the evolving working view.

8.2.2 Compilation and the program library

A Rational Environment view is not just a configuration of source elements; it is also a library. For each view the environment maintains an Ada program

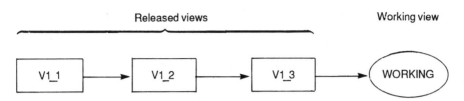

Figure 8.3   Released and working views of a Rational Environment subsystem

library derived from the source units in the view. Each Ada unit in a view is in one of three states: source, installed or coded.

- A *source* unit is produced using the Rational Environment syntax directed editor which ensures that it is syntactically correct Ada code.

- An *installed* unit has been compiled. It is available for compilation of units that depend upon it, and it is semantically consistent with units upon which it depends.

- A *coded* unit is ready for execution. The transition of the unit from the installed state to the coded state cannot fail; it simply requires time and computation.

A unit can be changed (within the check in, check out protocol) whatever its state. The state of the unit determines the degree of correctness which the changes must preserve. For example, changes to a source unit must be syntactically correct but need not be semantically correct.

Before changing a unit it is often necessary to demote other dependent units. For example, to change the specification of an Ada package other units which depend upon the specification might need to be demoted to the source state. The Rational Environment takes great care not to require the demotion of a unit unless absolutely necessary. For example, adding a procedure to a package specification is an upward compatible change and does not require that the units which depend upon the package are recompiled.

The Rational Environment provides a spectrum of approaches to compilation. At one end of the spectrum, the units in a working view are, whenever possible, installed or coded. Installed units are dynamically recompiled as they are changed, thereby providing immediate notification of semantic errors. The environment's knowledge of the unit's internal structure ensures that only those statements and declarations in the unit which have actually changed are recompiled. At the other end of the spectrum, units are held in the source state until they are installed and coded *en masse*. Knowledge of the dependencies between units always ensures that the units are compiled in a correct order. It is up to the engineer using the Rational Environment to decide which approach to use.

8.2.3 Subpaths for temporary variants

Figure 8.3 shows a linear path of views within a subsystem. More complex development paths are needed to manage variance. Figure 8.4 shows a development path with subpaths which provide working views for two developers. Anna and Bill create new element versions in the context of the working views Anna_working and Bill_working respectively. New versions are then accepted into the view Main_working for integration testing. After testing Main_working will be frozen as a release view.

There are two ways in which one working view is affected by changes made in the context of another working view. The first is if a working view explicitly accepts a new version of an element. For example, Main_working might accept a new element version developed by Anna in Anna_working; note that this does not affect Bill_working. The second is that when an element is checked out to a working view the latest version of the element is used. For example, if Anna checks in a new revision of an element to Anna_working and then Bill checks out the latest revision of that element to Bill_working then Bill acquires Anna's new revision.

The assumption so far has been that elements are *joined* between multiple working views in a subsystem; joined elements cannot be checked out to two working views at once. Exceptionally, an element in one view can sever all its links with the same element in other views. Severing a link creates a variant at the element level. The element can then be checked out to that view completely independently of other views. An element which has been severed can be rejoined by merging the changes that have been made to the severed copies.

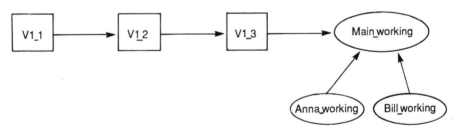

Figure 8.4   Variant subpaths for a Rational Environment subsystem

8.2.4 Paths for permanent variants

A subsystem which needs to exist as a set of permanent variants contains one path for each variant, each headed by a working view. Figure 8.5 shows two paths for a subsystem with a Unix and a VMS variant.

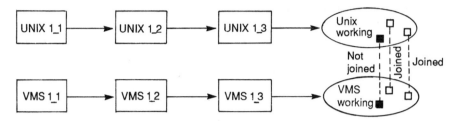

Figure 8.5   Variant paths for a Rational Environment subsystem

The Rational Environment manages permanent variance in essentially the same way that it manages temporary variance. The elements which are the same in the Unix and VMS variant of the subsystem are joined, whereas elements which need to differ between variants are severed. Joined elements cannot be checked out to Unix_working and VMS_working at the same time; changes made to a joined element in one working view will be accepted to the other when requested. On the other hand the severed elements in the two working views are completely independent of each other.

In many ways the Rational Environment's approach to managing variance is similar to DSEE's. Both use branch lines of descent for items which need to exist simultaneously in more than one version. However, DSEE only supports variant lines of descent for elements. Naming conventions for branches, such as those described in the DSEE case study, are needed so that a DSEE thread can define variant configurations. Rational Environment paths and subpaths represent variants explicitly at the subsystem level.

8.2.5 Subsystem interfaces

A view in the Rational Environment is either a *load view* or a *specification view*. The views discussed so far have all been load views; if the units in a load view are in the coded state then the view can be executed. A specification view, or spec view for short, represents the interface of a subsystem. A spec view is a subset of the specifications of the units in the subsystem and defines the units of the subsystem which are available to other subsystems.

Spec views and load views correspond at the subsystem level to Ada unit specifications and bodies at the element level. A load view implements a spec view in the same way that a unit body implements a unit specification. One subsystem imports a spec view of another in the same way that dependencies allow one Ada unit to use resources provided by another.

Figure 8.6 shows one subsystem dependent upon another. SUB_X, the client subsystem, imports the specification of unit B from the supplier subsystem SUB_Y upon which it depends. The supplier subsystem makes this unit available for compilation of load views in other subsystems by defining a spec view which contains the specification of B, but not of A or C. Spec views and load views support information hiding at the level above Ada packages: the Ada units A and C are entirely hidden from subsystem SUB_X.

Spec views also provide a boundary for recompilation requirements between subsystems. Changing the specification of unit B within the working (load) view of SUB_Y does not require recompilation in SUB_X, providing the change is compatible with the spec view. A load view is compatible with a spec view if it implements all the resources promised by the spec view.

In Figure 8.6 two release views, V2_1 and V2_2, and a working view all implement the spec view V2. The environment's version identification convention for subsystems is that a change to the subsystem interface, i.e. a new spec view, corresponds to a major release of a load view. For example, the spec view V3 will be implemented by load views V3_1, V3_2, etc.

8.2.6 Defining an executable system

Spec views allow one subsystem to compile against Ada specifications in another subsystem. Spec views cannot be executed. To execute the system one load view must be selected for each subsystem. In the Rational Environment this selection is defined by an *activity*. The nature of this selection depends upon the purpose of the activity, be it subsystem or integration testing or reconstructing a version of the system which has been issued to users.

The only constraint upon the load views selected by an activity is that the load view must be compatible with the spec view used to compile dependent load views in the activity. Of course, to execute the activity all units must be in the coded state.

The definition of subsystem views as a set of element versions, when combined with the definition of an activity as a set of subsystem versions, defines a configuration of the entire system. The Rational Environment's approach to defining subsystem versions is evolutionary: releases are defined as snapshots of working views which evolve as the subsystem's component elements evolve. Versions of the complete system, on the other hand, can be freely constructed as arbitrary combinations of compatible load views.

Figure 8.7 shows views of three subsystems of the database management system described in Chapter 3. The File Management subsystem has two development paths: one for the host Rational Environment and the other for the target Unix operating system. Each of the four activities uses an appropriate configuration of load views. For example, the activity for testing the working view of the Control Program uses stable released views of the Query Processing and File Management subsystems.

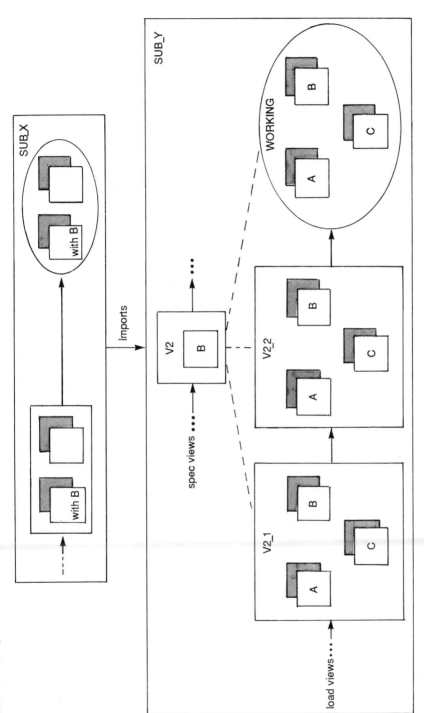

Figure 8.6   Subsystem interfaces using the Rational Environment

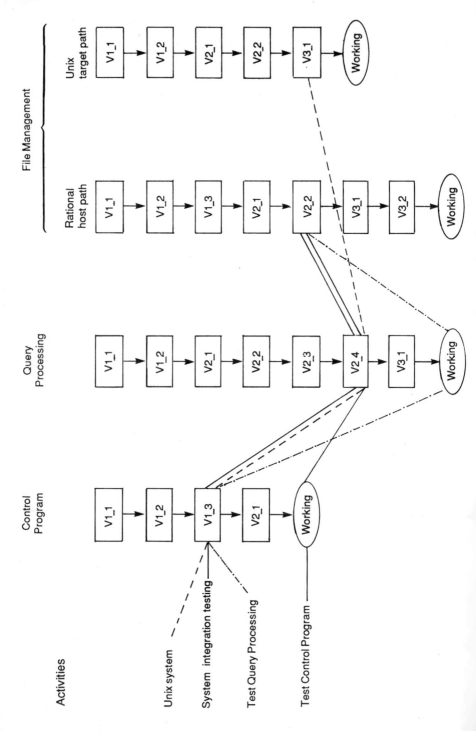

Figure 8.7 is superficially similar to Figure 3.1. A significant difference between the two figures is that the Rational Environment example describes configurations of subsystems whereas the earlier example describes configurations of elements within a single subsystem.

Key Points

- Ada distinguishes rigorously between the specification and the body of an element of code.

- The Ada program library captures the semantics of an Ada configuration. The library allows semantic checking between separately compiled elements of Ada code.

- These characteristics of Ada require the management of the library as a derived item and the careful control of when elements of Ada code are compiled and in what order.

- The Rational Environment divides a large system into subsystems which are further decomposed as elements. Ada provides information hiding at the element level; the Rational Environment provides information hiding at the subsystem level.

- The Rational Environment's smart recompilation facilities ensure that recompilation is kept to a minimum and that code is compiled in a correct order.

Figure 8.7   Activities using views of Rational Environment subsystems

9

CHANGE CONTROL

Change control is concerned with managing the process of developing and maintaining items, rather than managing the items which are the product of that process. Any change to an item of software is requested, evaluated, approved or rejected, scheduled and tracked. Change control (sometimes also called configuration control) provides explicit management procedures for each step in this process.

To many people change control suggests Byzantine clerical and administrative procedures which divert, and even inhibit, engineers from doing their job. Change control should not and need not be like that. It should be sensitive to the context in which it operates and, at any time, apply just the right degree of constraint on what an engineer can and cannot do.

It is true that change control requires an engineer to do more than just modify code. It requires the engineer to work in a responsible and disciplined way which contributes to the overall objectives of the team. This might sometimes involve filling in a form, or abstaining from last minute 'improvements' to software which is about to be released. A little bureaucracy is, however, a small price to pay for the benefits of change control which ensures that:

- There is a well-defined procedure for requesting a change and implementing the change if the request is approved.

- The implementation of an approved change can be planned with regard to its importance, its impact and the resources it requires.

- Changing an item does not have unexpected and adverse side effects.

- The status of a request for change and of the items to which it refers is documented.

The first two sections of this chapter describe the CM framework in which an item is reviewed and approved. Subsequent sections describe how changes to approved items are requested, evaluated and implemented.

9.1 THE LIFECYCLE OF AN ITEM

Figure 9.1 is a simple model of the lifecycle of one version of a software item. While the status of an item is working it can be freely changed by its developer. When work on the item is complete it is reviewed. As soon as the item's status is promoted from working to under review it is frozen. This version of the item can no longer be amended by its developer or by anyone else; the only way to change it is to create a new version. When the item is under review it is the responsibility of the review authority either to approve the item or to reject it as unfit for its intended purpose. This generic lifecycle applies to all types of item: source code and documentation; an element of code or a version of the entire system.

Figure 9.1   The generic lifecycle of an item version

The status of a derived element is the same as the source element from which it is built. If a derived element is built from several source elements then its status is that of the least approved of its sources. By similar principles, the status of a composite item cannot be greater than the status of any of its components. It is meaningless to review an item which contains elements that are not frozen—what is being reviewed? Equally it would be folly to approve a configuration which contains elements that have not been approved.

In practice, the generic lifecycle varies greatly with the type of item and the size and complexity of the system of which it is a part. Figure 9.2 shows a typical lifecycle of an element of source code.

Figure 9.2   The lifecycle of an element of code

Of course an item may fail a review at any stage of its lifecycle. In Figures 9.1 and 9.2 these contingencies are not explicitly shown. Figure 9.3 shows the lifecycle of one version of a complete system; it defines a state for the system should it fail either alpha or beta testing.

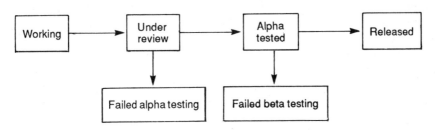

Figure 9.3   The lifecycle of a system

The status of an item should be recorded with the item's identification. This is common practice for documents: a document front sheet typically records whether the document is frozen and, if so, whether it has been approved. A similar approach should be adopted for all types of item.

The traditional role of the software library is that of a repository for fully approved items. A somewhat broader view of the library's role is that it should hold all items as soon as they are frozen; this is the sort of library provided by tools like SCCS and CMS. Some modern CM tools provide a working version of an item which can be amended without creating a new version. Recall, for example, how in the Rational Environment a release view is created as a snapshot of a working view. Later chapters describe how PCMS and PCTE manage working, mutable versions of items.

Many CM tools provide facilities for recording the evolution of an item through its lifecycle. Lifespan supports the basic lifecycle of Figure 9.1. CCC and PCMS provide facilities for tailoring an item's lifecycle to meet the particular needs the project and, in the case of PCMS, of the type of item. CCC is also supplied as CCC/DM, a turnkey system for development and maintenance in which all items have a fixed lifecycle. These tools are described in more detail in Chapter 10.

9.2 REVIEWS AND THE CONFIGURATION CONTROL BOARD

Each step in the promotion of an item version through its lifecycle is the consequence of a review which approves the item. The ultimate authority for the integrity of items is the *configuration control board*, or CCB. The CCB is responsible for the approval of items and for judging whether a proposed change to an approved item is desirable. Despite its grand title, for a small project the role of CCB is often fulfilled by a single person such as the project manager. In many organisations the CCB is known by another title, for example review board, change control board or quality control.

A well-constituted CCB should not and need not be heavy handed or bureaucratic. The CCB usually delegates its authority and responsibility, particularly for the early stages of the review process. For example, a single author is usually responsible for writing a design document and for deciding when the document is ready for its initial review, perhaps by a small design team; if the document passes its initial review it is then reviewed more widely, perhaps by representatives of related design teams or perhaps by users of the system. Later sections of this chapter describe how the CCB may be organised.

The process by which an item is reviewed varies enormously with the type of item and the required level of integrity. In general a review investigates whether:

- The item conforms to its specification (*verification*).

- The item meets the expectations of its users, whether or not these expectations are explicit in the item's specification (*validation*).

- For a composite item, all the components of the item are present and correct (*configuration audit*).

- The item complies with the project's quality standards.

Review techniques include:

- *Inspection.* In the right circumstances, engineers are very good at detecting errors. [Fagan 76] and [Fagan 86] describe a disciplined way of organising the inspection of an item. Fagan's recommendations include that material should be distributed to reviewers prior to the inspection, that reviewers should be assigned roles such as 'user' or 'maintainer', that the objective of a review is to find errors, not to correct them, and that a review should not be diverted by questions of style.

- *Dynamic testing.* An item of code can be tested by executing the code and looking for unexpected behaviour. [Meyers 79] describes techniques for selecting test data.

- *Automatic static analysis.* Tools can detect certain types of error in an item, for example that a document is not in the format required by the quality standards or that an element of source code contains syntax errors. Some CM tools analyse an element when requested to check the element into the software library; if the element fails its analysis then it is not checked in.

- *Formal verification.* If an item is specified precisely then the implementation of the item can be proved to be mathematically correct. [Cohen 86] provides an introduction to such techniques.

The details of these techniques are not described further. The objective here is to describe a framework within which items are reviewed at appropriate stages of their lifecycle. CM ensures that no item slips through the net of critical review, that an item under review is frozen and uniquely identified and that the result of each review is clearly recorded.

9.3 THE NEED FOR CHANGE CONTROL

9.3.1 The need for change

In an ideal world, once an item is fully approved there would be no need to change it. In the real world new versions are needed for a variety of reasons:

- The requirements for the system change. The market for a software product may change or the requirements for a bespoke system may be redefined.

- The boundaries between items in the design hierarchy change. The precise interface between items may need to be renegotiated as software is designed and written. This requires changes to the specification of items.

- The specification of an item is incomplete or wrongly interpreted. Writing software often involves making judgements about what the specification really means. Although an item is correct for one interpretation of its specification, it may transpire that a different interpretation was intended.

- An error is found that was not detected during the item's review. No review mechanism is foolproof; some faults always slip through the most rigorous review.

- The software environment changes in a way that necessitates change. For example, a new version of a compiler may be less tolerant of deviations from standard features of the programming language.

In each of these cases a new revision of an item is needed which supersedes the earlier revision. Replacing one version of an item with a better one is the objective of all change. One of the problems of change is that what is better in one context may prove to be disastrously worse in another.

9.3.2 The need for control

Anna has written a routine which sorts a list of names into alphabetical order. The routine works well and is used extensively throughout the rest of the system. One evening Anna reads [Knuth 73] and learns that the bubble sort algorithm she has used is actually very inefficient and that a Shell sort is much faster. What happens next? In the absence of proper change control, almost anything might! Some of the possibilities include:

- Anna replaces the old bubble sort with a Shell sort; she does not have time to test the routine which fails 99% of the time. All hell breaks loose in the development team after the next build of the system.

- Anna replaces the old bubble sort with a Shell sort which fails one percent of the time when an addressing error corrupts memory. The system then fails unaccountably while performing a function which is unrelated to the sort routine.

- Anna spends the next week coding and testing the Shell sort. Unfortunately, she does not manage to finish the crucial work she ought to be doing. The sort routine runs slightly faster, but the project is a week late.

- Anna replaces the old bubble sort with a Shell sort. For randomly ordered data the Shell sort is a lot quicker. Unfortunately the data passed to the sort routine is usually roughly in order already. For such data a bubble sort is actually much quicker than a Shell sort.

- Anna recognises all the dangers of changing an element which has been approved, and does nothing. The idea of using a more efficient sort algorithm is forgotten.

   The problem of Anna and her sort routine is an example of change from the bottom up; it illustrates several but by no means all of the problems of change. Change can also be prompted from the top. Consider the problems of Bill, the project manager for the development of the payroll system described in Chapter 4. The project is proceeding smoothly: the functionality of the system has been agreed; the system has been divided into subsystems, each of which is being developed by separate teams. One morning Sally, the marketing vice-president, calls Bill into her office and suggests a list of changes which will help to sell the system. 'Suggests' is Sally's word, but Bill knows what she really means.
   Bill reads Sally's list of changes with growing dismay. Some affect just one subsystem, others require coordinated changes to several subsystems. Some

of the changes look quite trivial but actually require a significant redesign which would delay the first version of the payroll system by several weeks. Bill has no idea what is involved in making some of the changes; he needs to consult engineers with a more detailed knowledge of a particular component of the payroll system. Some of the changes look good in isolation but are incompatible with the rest of the system.

How should Bill cope with Sally's requests for change? For each change Bill needs to know why the change has been proposed, the impact of the change and the implementation cost. If Sally is prepared to bear the cost of a change Bill needs to be able to control its implementation. Bill needs a framework for managing change; he needs change control.

9.4 THE PRINCIPLES OF CHANGE CONTROL

9.4.1 The change lifecycle

All software projects need change control; however, the level and formality of control required varies considerably. Changes to fully approved items in a large system need strict and formal change control. A small team developing a research prototype can rely on less formal control.

Whatever the context, change control must always provide:

- A channel through which a change can be requested.

- A mechanism for evaluating the change which takes account of its cost and effect on other items.

- An authority responsible for approving or rejecting the change.

- A method of tracking the change from its request to its implementation.

Figure 9.4 shows the generic lifecycle of a *Change Request*, or *CR*. There is a close relationship between this diagram and Figure 9.1 which showed the

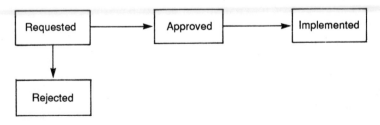

Figure 9.4   The generic lifecycle of a change request

generic lifecycle for an item version: the criterion for approving an item version is that it is an acceptable implementation of a request for change.

9.4.2 A simple change request form

The status of a CR is often recorded by a single document called a CR form. Fields of the CR form are filled in as the change progresses through its lifecycle. Chapter 10 discusses how change control can be automated and how CRs can be managed by CM tools; this chapter concentrates on paper based approaches.

Figure 9.5 is a simple example of a CR form. Every organisation has its own CR form which is tailored to meet its requirements, if only by decorating the form with the company logo! All CR forms should allow continuation sheets so that the amount of information which can be supplied is not limited by the size of the form. The three main areas of the form shown as Figure 9.5 correspond to the three stages of the change lifecycle: requested, approved and implemented.

The first area of the form describes the requested change; it is completed by the originator of the CR. The item to be changed is an item in the hierarchy which contains all the items to be changed. If the change affects several subsystems or if the originator does not know about the item structure of the system, then the CR cites the entire system. The next two fields describe how and why the item should be changed. The aim here should be to describe the effect of the change, rather than precisely how that effect is achieved. For example, a CR which reports a fault should describe very precisely the circumstances in which the fault occurs but should not speculate about how the fault may be corrected. Similarly, a request for an enhancement to an item should be accompanied by a description of the new functionality and why it is needed.

The originator of the CR must be recorded so that he or she can be informed of the progress of the CR through its lifecycle. The originator will wish to receive an acknowledgement of the CR, to know whether the request is approved or rejected and, if approved, when it is implemented. He or she may also need to be consulted for further information, for example about a fault that cannot be reproduced.

Once the first area of the CR form is completed, the CR is registered in the change control system. The CR is immediately assigned an identification number which is recorded at the top of the form. Usually a CR is identified by the next available integer in a continuous sequence.

The CR is then reviewed by the CCB. This aspect of the CCB's role is described in detail in Section 6.5. The second area of the CR form records the results of the CCB's deliberations. If the CR is rejected, the reason why should

```
┌─────────────────────────────────────────────────────────────────┐
│                                                                   │
│        Change Request              CR id :                        │
│                                                                   │
├───────────────────────────────────────────────────────────────── │
│                            To be completed by originator          │
│     Item to be changed:              Version:                     │
│                                                                   │
│     Description of change:                                        │
│                                                                   │
│                                                                   │
│     Reason for change:                                            │
│                                                                   │
│     Originator:                        Date:                      │
├───────────────────────────────────────────────────────────────── │
│                            To be completed by CCB                 │
│     CR approved/rejected       Authority:          Date:          │
│                                                                   │
│     Comments:                                                     │
│                                                                   │
│                                                                   │
│                                                                   │
│                                                                   │
├───────────────────────────────────────────────────────────────── │
│                            To be completed by implementor         │
│     Change implemented in items :         Version:                │
│                                                                   │
│     Comments:                                                     │
│                                                                   │
│                                                                   │
└─────────────────────────────────────────────────────────────────┘
```

Figure 9.5   A simple change request form

always be recorded. If the CR is approved, the CCB may wish to constrain how the change is implemented; for example, the CCB may require that the change is implemented by a certain date or that the items are changed in a certain way.

The third and last area of the CR form records the implementation of the CR as a new version of an item. It provides answers to questions like 'Has the CR number 123 been implemented in the version 2.1 of the system?' The field for comments allows the implementer to provide further details about how the change is implemented, for example to list the revised elements.

9.4.3 Using the simple change request form in practice

The CR form described above is simple, informal and flexible. It works well for a small software project of up to roughly ten engineers. The form contains only a few fields; the meaning of some of these fields is not precisely defined but is left to the common sense of whoever fills in the form. The form is suitable for all types of item, and may be used either to request an enhancement or to report a fault.

Anyone connected with a software project, from the most junior programmer to the client, should be able to raise a CR. This is not just egalitarian, it is sensible. People with different roles have different viewpoints and can all make valuable proposals as to how the system may be improved. Of course it is open to the CCB to pay more heed to CRs which originate from a paying client than from a programmer!

The smooth operation of a change control system, especially for occasional users of the system, is greatly improved by guidelines for its use. The guidelines should cover the sort of issues discussed in Section 9.4.2 as well as administrative details such as how to use continuation sheets and how the CR is entered into the change control system. The guidelines should be concise and may be copied on the back of every paper CR form or supplied as help text for an electronic form.

A paper based change control system is inefficient for a large project. The volume of paper generated by copying a CR to all interested parties at each stage of its lifecycle soon becomes overwhelming. Also, much time can be wasted searching through files of CRs, for example for those CRs which affect a particular subsystem. A paper based system is adequate when the number of CRs is measured in hundreds; if there are thousands of CRs an automated system of the kind described in Chapter 10 is almost essential.

9.5 THE REVIEW OF A CR BY THE CCB

This section describes in more detail the composition of the CCB and its responsibilities for change control. Except for a small project, it is inefficient for the same person or group of people to review all CRs; the section concludes with a summary of how CCBs may be structured hierarchically so that each CR is reviewed by the appropriate people.

9.5.1 The function of the CCB

The CCB decides whether a CR should be approved or rejected. To make this judgement the CCB must answer the following four questions:

- *What is the extent of the requested change?* If an item is to be changed then any other item which depends upon it may also need to be changed. For example, the effect of a change to an element of source code may ripple through all the code in the system; it may also require changes to the system and user documentation. The CCB must be aware of all these implications. This question is much easier to address if the system is structured so that dependencies are minimised and are explicit.

- *What is the cost of the change?* The resources needed to implement the change must be estimated, as well as the effect of allocating these resources on the project's plan and budget. The most significant cost is usually the time it would take to implement the change.

- *What are the advantages and disadvantages of the change?* Several perspectives are needed to answer this question. Clearly the user perspective is important, but so too is the perspective of the engineers who must maintain the system and the designers who are responsible for its long term evolution. For example, there is little to be gained by implementing a small enhancement to a part of the system which will be completely rewritten for the next major release.

- *How important is the change?* As well as deciding whether the change constitutes a net improvement to the system, the CCB must quantify its importance and urgency. A CR may be an elegant idea, with no disadvantages, but with no significant benefits either! Conversely, a change to the payroll system may be clumsy and fraught with difficulty, but essential for the beginning of the next financial year.

These questions are called *impact analysis*. If the CCB is large or the CR is complex, then the first two questions may be the subject of an initial investigation which presents its findings to the CCB. As well as recording whether the CR is approved, the CCB should also summarise the principal conclusions of its impact analysis. Using the simple CR form shown in Figure 9.5 this information would be written in the comments field of the second area of the form.

The CCB is not usually responsible for planning the implementation of an approved change. In principle the CCB's role is judicial, not executive. In practice, the CCB often exerts some control on how a change is implemented. The boundary between the CCB and the project manager responsible for implementing approved changes is discussed in Section 9.7.

The CCB's responsibility for a CR continues after it approves the CR; it only ends when the CCB approves a version of an item which implements the CR. Although the CCB is likely to delegate its authority for reviewing the implementation of the CR, the principle is important: the CCB must not approve a CR and then wash its hands of the matter.

9.5.2 The composition of the CCB

The CCB must decide whether the benefits of a CR justify its cost. To do so, it needs both authority and expertise. The CCB must be able to allocate the resources needed to implement a change; a CCB which can only discuss or review CRs but cannot commit resources is no more than a talking shop. To judge whether a CR should be approved the CCB must represent everyone with a legitimate interest in the proposed change:

- *Users of the system.* The objective of a software system is to meet the requirements of its users. Changes to approved items must take account of the needs of the system's users. For bespoke software a change to the system may imply a change to the contract between the supplier and client; it would be suicidal for the supplier to make such a change without the client's written agreement.

- *The technical authority for the system.* The CCB must be fully aware of the technical implications of the proposed change. Someone with detailed knowledge of the system design is needed to assess precisely what the change involves.

- *The project manager.* If a CR is approved, it is the project manager who will be responsible for its implementation. The project manager ensures that the deliberations of the CCB are realistic and pragmatic. For example, if implementing the CR would delay the next release of the system, then the project manager must make this very clear to the other members of the CCB.

By now the reader may feel intimidated by the concept of a CCB: by its grand title, its authority and its apparent size. In fact a CCB of some kind is essential for even the smallest project. For a small project the roles which the CCB must represent (user, designer, manager) may coincide in a single person. Conversely, for a large project the CCB may include several users of the system. For example, in the CCB for the payroll system the role of user might encompass the marketing vice-president responsible for selling the system, the manager of the payroll department of a potential client and a data entry clerk who will actually use the payroll system.

The constitution of the CCB varies enormously from project to project. It must always be clearly defined by terms of reference which describe the

CCB's membership, its powers and the principles of how it operates, for example how frequently it meets and how disagreements between its members are resolved. The terms of reference of the CCB form part of a project's CM plan, as described in Chapter 12.

9.5.3 The hierarchy of CCBs

Except for a small project, it is not usually necessary for a single CCB to review all CRs. Some CRs have considerable impact and need to be reviewed by the full CCB; others have limited impact and would waste the time of most members of the CCB. The solution to this problem is to have not one CCB but a hierarchy of CCBs. The structure of this hierarchy corresponds roughly to the higher levels of the design item hierarchy for the system.

To illustrate this approach, consider how changes to the ACOMP compiler may be reviewed. The design item hierarchy for this system is shown in Figure 9.6. The ACOMP system comprises three subsystems: LEX the lexical analyser, PARSER the syntax analyser and CODEGEN the code generator.

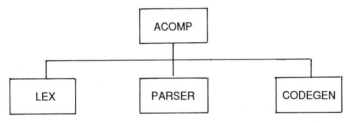

Figure 9.6   The design item hierarchy for the ACOMP compiler

Figure 9.7 shows the five CCBs for this system. CCB/LEX, CCB/PARSER and CCB/CODEGEN review CRs which affect the implementation of the corresponding subsystem but not its interface. A CR which affects more than one subsystem but does not affect the specification of the ACOMP compiler is reviewed by CCB/ACOMP, for example a change to the LEX subsystem which also requires changes to the PARSER subsystem. A change to the specification of the ACOMP system, for example a change to the syntax of the ACOMP language, is reviewed by CCB/CLIENT.

The five CCBs all function according to the same principles, but they function at different levels. For example, the roles of user, designer and manager are interpreted differently for each CCB. In CCB/LEX the role of user represents the engineers developing the LEX subsystem who depend upon the element to be changed; in CCB/CLIENT the user is the client who is paying for the system.

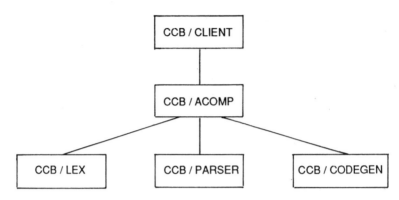

Figure 9.7   A hierarchy of CCBs for the ACOMP compiler

Following [Dowson 87], each CCB may be regarded as controlling a contract which defines the services that one item of software provides to another. For a bespoke system there is usually a legal contract between the software supplier and the client. If the three subsystems of the ACOMP compiler are developed by subcontractors, then the specification of each subsystem is also the subject of a legal contract between the subcontractor and the prime contractor. At the lower and less formal levels of the CCB hierarchy, the contracts are less likely to be legally binding.

How do change control procedures ensure that each CR is reviewed at the right level? A CR identifies the item to be changed which in turn indicates the CCB which should first consider the CR. The CR then filters up the hierarchy of CCBs until it reaches the right level. For example, a request to change the LEX subsystem, or a component element of this subsystem, would in the first instance be reviewed by CCB/LEX. This CCB may decide that the requested change affects the interface of the LEX subsystem as well as its implementation; if so then CCB/LEX passes the CR up to CCB/ACOMP. If CCB/ACOMP decides that the CR affects the specification of the ACOMP system then the CR is passed up another level to CCB/CLIENT.

9.6 FAULT REPORTING

Previous sections of this chapter have outlined a general approach to change control in which one type of CR form is used for all requests for change. In practice there are different types of CR. Some are urgent, others less so. Some are raised within the organisation responsible for developing and maintaining the software, others are raised by users outside this organisation. Probably the most significant distinction between CRs is whether the CR requests an enhancement or reports a fault. This section discusses CRs which report a fault. Such a CR is variously known as an incident, trouble, defect, anomaly, observation, bug or fault report. This book will use the term *Fault Report*, or *FR* for short.

9.6.1 The content of a fault report

The primary objective of an FR is to provide the information about the item which is needed to identify the fault. The secondary objective is to highlight the effect of fault. In general, an FR should not describe how the software should be changed to fix the fault. When a patient visits her doctor she does not announce that she needs a certain drug, she describes her symptoms; the doctor then prescribes an appropriate treatment. Similarly the change requested by a FR is to fix the fault; how the fix is achieved should not concern the originator of the FR. An FR must describe:

- *The full identity of the item exhibiting the fault.* The CCB must review an FR by referring to a particular version of an item. The fault might already be fixed in the most recent revision of the item, or the fault may not be fixed but the item may have been revised so that the fault occurs in different circumstances. It is not sufficient for an FR to imply that the fault occurs in the most recent version of the item (which is ambiguous) or in all versions (which might not be true).

- *The nature of the fault.* An FR should state clearly how the behaviour of the item is faulty. The FR may need to refer to documentation which describes how the item should behave, for example a user manual or the item's specification, as evidence of a fault. The CCB may then deem the fault to be in the documentation, not the item itself.

- *The circumstances in which the fault occurred.* An FR should describe precisely and completely the inputs to which the item responds incorrectly. This description will vary with the type of item and the fault. For example, an FR for the ACOMP compiler should include the source text which exposes the fault and the options passed to the compiler; on the other hand, a fault in a wordprocessor may be described by a sequence of user operations which reveals a fault independently of the document which is being updated.

- *The environment in which the fault occurred.* A range of factors which are not obviously connected with the item at fault may affect its behaviour, for example the operating system platform and hardware configuration, the date and time, and other software which shares resources with the faulty item. Any of these factors may provide vital clues in tracking down the cause of a fault.

- *Diagnostic information.* An item may detect its own failure and then provide information which helps to diagnose the cause of the failure. An item may provide, for example, a system error code, a memory dump or a traceback of its recent operation.

- *The effect of the fault.* An FR should describe the originator's assessment of the consequence of the fault. The orginator may, from bitter experience, be able to highlight a consequence which is not immediately apparent. Quantitative ways of indicating the importance of an FR are discussed in Section 9.6.3.

The relative importance of these parts of an FR varies with the fault and the item. A good FR form prompts the originator to supply the appropriate information, but ultimately it is up to the originator herself to judge just what is and what is not important. A practical consideration which affects this question is how easy it is to obtain further information should it be needed. If the originator is a client in another continent, the FR must include every scrap of information that might be useful; conversely, if the project is small and the originator shares an office with the engineer who will investigate the fault, then the FR can afford to be less comprehensive.

9.6.2 Change control procedures for fault reports

It is clear that there are significant differences between a fault report and a request for enhancement. How should these differences affect change control procedures? It is quite possible to use the same change control procedure for both faults and enhancements. Indeed there is an important advantage to such an approach: it is not always clear whether a CR should be regarded as a fault report or an enhancement request. Consider a request that the ACOMP compiler should provide a more helpful error message for a certain syntax error. Is this a fault report or an enhancement request? If the behaviour of all software items is always precisely and completely specified then this ambiguity would not arise. In practice, this is rarely the case, especially for software concerned with the user interface of a system.

A separate procedure for reporting faults is most useful during the maintenance phase of a project. In this phase the expected behaviour of the software is well understood so it is easier to distinguish between a fault report and an enhancement request. There may also be separate teams responsible for fixing faults in released software and performing the enhancements needed for the next major release.

Figure 9.8 is an example of a form for reporting faults; it supports the change lifecycle of Figure 9.9. The lifecycle includes one more stage than the

Fault Report	FR id:

To be completed by originator

Item: Version:

Description of fault (include available diagnostics):

Circumstance and environment of fault:

Effect of fault:

Priority: Originator: Date:

To be completed by investigator

Cause of fault:

Proposed fix:

Estimated cost of fix (work days):

Priority: Investigator: Date:

To be completed by CCB

FR approved/rejected   Priority: Authority: Date:

Comments:

To be completed by implementor

Change implemented in item: Version:

Comments:

Figure 9.8   A fault report form

generic change lifecycle of Figure 9.4. In this stage the fault is investigated before the CCB approves a change which fixes the fault. The four main areas of the FR form correspond to the four main stages of the lifecycle. The first area is completed by the originator; it provides all the information discussed in Section 9.6.1. The second area is completed by the investigator who identifies the cause of the fault, proposes a fix and makes an initial estimate of the cost of the fix. The investigator may conclude that the reported fault is

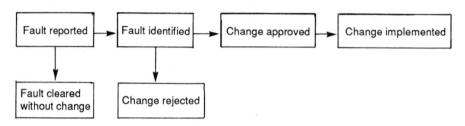

Figure 9.9   The lifecycle of a fault report

not really a fault at all; for example, it may arise from a misunderstanding by the originator of how the item should behave—in this case the FR is cleared without change to the software. The last two areas are similar to the last two areas of the CR form of Figure 9.5.

9.6.3 The priority of a fault

It is useful for a CR, and particularly for an FR, to describe how urgently the change is needed. The information is useful:

- As input to planning the implementation of the change, so that high priority fixes or enhancements may be allocated more resources.

- To drive the change control process itself. For example, the CCB may be constituted so that it is required to respond to each high priority FR within a week of its receipt.

- As an indication of the quality of an item measured by the number of outstanding faults recorded against it and the priority of these faults.

There are many ways of designating the priority of a fault. The most effective take account of the type of item in question. For example, a documentation fault might be designated as 'typographical', 'unclear', 'incomplete', 'misleading' or 'incorrect' whereas a fault in a flight control system might be categorised according to whether of not it is 'flight limiting'.

There are more general ways of designating the priority of a fault, for example as high, medium or low, or on a scale of one to ten. The problem with such approaches is that they are ambiguous: the designation of a fault's priority may depend upon the temper of the originator of the FR as much as anything else! The most effective general approach is for the priority of the fault to indicate the consequences if the fault is not fixed. For example, a fault may be categorised according to whether it:

- Renders the entire system unusable.

- Renders one or more functions provided by the system unusable.

- Can be worked around, but not easily.

- Has no significant effect upon the utility of the system.

Who should assess the priority of a fault? Certainly the originator of the FR should assess its significance. If the lifecycle of an FR is as shown in Figure 9.9 then either or both of the investigator and the CCB may wish to modify the originator's priority. For example, the investigator may determine that the cause of the fault has more serious implications than that noticed by the originator, or the CCB may judge that the fault is not really as important as has been asserted by the originator. The FR form shown in Figure 9.8 allows each of the originator, the investigator and the CCB to assess the priority of the fault.

9.7 IMPLEMENTING CHANGE

The implementation of change lies on the border between CM and project management. It involves identifying packages of work, scheduling these workpackages, assigning them to appropriately qualified engineers, monitoring progress and controlling quality. Much of this is beyond the scope of CM. This section discusses aspects of software project management which are important for managing the implementation of approved changes.

9.7.1 The boundary between the CCB and the project manager

The CCB is responsible for approving or rejecting a CR and for monitoring its implementation if it is approved. The project manager is responsible for managing the implementation of the CR. The boundary between the CCB and the project manager varies from project to project, but it must always be precisely defined. Each must be aware of the other's responsibilities and powers. The CCB must not demand changes which the project manager does not have the resources to implement, whereas the project manager must be required to implement changes approved by the CCB. The following is one way to draw the boundary between the CCB and the project manager:

- *CCB responsibilities.* For each approved CR, the CCB specifies the date by which the change must be implemented and the agreed cost of implementation. The due date is often related to a project milestone, for example the next release of the system. The due date may be left open for CRs which the CCB judges to be not urgent.

- *Project manager responsibilities.* The project manager is required to implement an approved CR by the due date and using the resources specified by the CCB. The project manager is a member of the CCB and has therefore agreed the cost of implementing the change.

Change Request   CR id:

To be completed by originator

Item to be changed: Version:

This CR reports a fault/requests an enhancement

Description of change:

Reason for change:

Priority: Originator: Date:

To be completed by CCB

CR approved/rejected   Authority: Date:

Estimated cost of change (work days):

Change required by:

Comments:

To be completed by implementor

Change implemented in item: Version:

Implementation approved by quality control authority: Date:

Comments:

Figure 9.10   A more sophisticated change request form

Figure 9.10 is a more elaborate version of the simple CR form shown as Figure 9.5. It includes fields which support this division of responsibilities between the CCB and the project manager. Alternatively, the information contained in the extra fields of this form can be included in the comment fields of the simpler form. Variations of this approach may be used as circumstances demand; for example, the CCB may require a certain proportion of changes which are not urgent to be made by a particular time.

9.7.2 Workpackages for change

A *workpackage* is a unit of work which may be assigned to one or more engineers. By accepting responsibility for the workpackage the engineer undertakes to perform the work at an agreed cost, often defined by the date when the work must be complete. For further discussion of workpackages see [Ould 90].

Like any other task which a project must perform, a change to an approved item must be the subject of one or more workpackages. There are several ways of allocating change implementations to workpackages. The cost of the change largely determines which of the four approaches listed below is most appropriate.

- *An on-going workpackage to cover minor changes.* A team of engineers may be responsible both for development work for the next release of the system and for fixing faults in the most recent release. The effort needed to implement minor changes can be scheduled as an on-going workpackage which has no end date but is resourced at a fixed level, for example two days from each engineer per month.

- *Extending an existing workpackage.* The project manager may modify an existing workpackage so that it incorporates the implementation of one or more related changes. The cost of the workpackage is also modified and the revision to the workpackage is agreed by the responsible engineer.

- *Defining a new workpackage for one or more changes.* The project manager may group one or more related changes into a workpackage which implements the changes.

- *Managing a change as a subproject.* A major change constitutes an increment to the system which must be specified, designed and coded as a project in its own right. Such a change requires several workpackages and several intermediate reviews before its implementation is complete.

The lifecycle for a CR and the lifecycle for a new version of an item both conclude with the CCB's approval of the item version which implements the change. A *change authorisation* form may be used to formally approve items which implement one or more CRs. At a minimum this form records the new item versions which it approves and the CRs which these items implement. If change authorisation forms are used then the implementation area of the CR form should reference the change authorisation which approves the items that implement the change. [IEEE-1042 87] contains several examples of change authorisation forms.

9.7.3 Adopting revised items

When a new version of an item is approved it is checked into the software library. The item can then be used as a component of other configurations. In particular, it may be adopted by other members of the project team to test their work.

For example, suppose Anna has revised the SORT routine: version 2.3 of this element uses a bubble sort whereas the most recent version in the library, version 2.4, uses a Shell sort. Chris, who is testing his working version of the REPORT subsystem, may wish to continue to use version 2.3 of the SORT routine; he wants to be confident that any problems with his working version of the REPORT subsystem are nothing to do with the items which the REPORT subsystem uses. On the other hand, once Chris is happy with the new version of the REPORT subsystem he will wish to test it with the latest version of all the items it uses.

The CM tools discussed in Chapters 6, 7 and 8 allow Chris to work in this way. Configurations may be specified which use either a specific, frozen version of an item or the latest version. A danger with this flexibility is that Chris may continue to use the out of date version of the SORT routine indefinitely. A prudent manager will encourage the project team to use the most up to date items in the software library, for example by legislating that engineers must not use an out of date version of an item for longer than a month.

9.7.4 Synchronising changes

Frequently the implementation of a change requires the revision of several items. For example, if the number of arguments to a routine is changed then all the elements which use that routine must be changed as well as the routine itself. The problem for change control is to ensure that configurations contain either all of the elements which have been revised or none of them. If engineers build configurations using the most recent versions of all elements of the library then all the revised elements must be replaced in the library at the same time. If engineers are able to select flexibly the elements of a configuration, as they are using DSEE or the Rational Environment, then a method is needed which ensures that either all or none of the elements which have been revised as part of a change are used in any configuration. The DSEE case study described in Chapter 7 is an example of such a method.

9.8 CHANGE CONTROL IN PRACTICE

The principles of change control described in this chapter can be implemented to provide greater or lesser levels of control. Providing the correct level of change control is probably the greatest CM challenge a project has to face. If change control is too restrictive then the bureaucracy of change swamps the effort needed to perform the change, so nothing gets done. If change control is too weak then engineers chase their own tails in a frustrating, unstable and undisciplined environment.

This section discusses a range of factors which determine the appropriate level of change control. The abstraction which underlies each of these factors is the impact of change: if a change has a great impact then the change must be rigorously controlled; if a change has little impact then it should be controlled informally.

9.8.1 The size of the project team

The single most important factor which affects the correct level of change control is the number of engineers with a legitimate interest in the change. A small project team usually enjoys good informal communication between its members. It can therefore rely to a large extent on flexible and informal change control. A team of up to five engineers, such as the chief programmer team described in [Brooks 75], can use the simple CR of Figure 9.5 with the chief programmer fulfilling the role of CCB. Changes which only affect members of the project team are reviewed by the chief programmer as they arise.

A larger project team, especially if it is distributed between several locations, must use more formal procedures. A request for change must be more precise, the CCB must comprise more than just one person and the CCB must meet regularly. A large project should be divided into parts, each with its own CCB, which are related hierarchically in the way outlined in Section 9.5.3.

9.8.2 The level of approval of the item to be changed

The level of change control needed to supersede an item with a new revision must increase with the level of approval which the earlier revision has achieved. For example, a draft version of a document may be superseded after informal discussions within the project team; once the document has been approved it should only be changed with CCB approval.

The ACOMP compiler provides another example of the same principle. The compiler comprises the three subsystems illustrated in Figure 9.6. Each subsystem is developed by a team which is responsible for testing its subsystem independently of the other two. Figure 9.11 summarises the lifecycle of a version of the LEX subsystem. The authority responsible for each promotion is shown above each transition; for example, CCB/LEX approves a new revision of LEX as being subsystem tested.

Figure 9.11   The lifecycle of a version of the LEX subsystem

The level of promotion achieved by the subsystem defines the authority needed to approve changes to it. Thus if LEX has been subsystem tested but not integration tested, then changes must be approved by CCB/LEX but need not concern CCB/ACOMP. Similarly CCB/CLIENT does not need to approve a change until the software has released status. A change is the concern of a CCB if, and only if, that CCB has previously approved the item to be changed.

For small projects, change to an item may be informally controlled until the item is approved, at which time formal change control is imposed. For larger projects, like the ACOMP compiler, items are promoted through levels of approval and visibility. As an item is promoted, the impact of a change to the item increases and so does the need for formal change control.

9.8.3 Experimental changes

Suppose that integration testing of the ACOMP compiler reveals a fault in the LEX subsystem. The fault is so serious that it stops further integration testing, but it appears to be easy to fix. The normal procedure for fixing the fault is to raise an FR which is then investigated, reviewed by the CCB and then implemented by the LEX development team before the fix is at last available to the integration team. However, grinding through this procedure for each fault would bring integration testing to a standstill! What is to be done?

Change control must provide a procedure for making experimental or emergency changes quickly. For experimental changes to the ACOMP compiler by the integration team an informal integration CCB may be constituted, or experimental changes might be permitted without formal change control. Item versions created by the integration team are designated to be of experimental status. By the principle that an item cannot be of higher status than any item it contains, any configuration which contains an item of experimental status is itself experimental.

Making an experimental change is perfectly consistent with sound change control. The key question is what happens next. An experimental item fulfils a temporary but urgent need—in the example of the ACOMP compiler, to allow integration testing to continue. An experimental item should not be issued to users and should not be the basis of further change, except further experimental change. All faults found during integration of the ACOMP compiler should be recorded with an FR. If an experimental change seems to fix the fault then the integration team must check this experimental item into the library as a temporary variant with experimental status. The FR should refer to this experimental item as a possible way of fixing the fault. The FR is then resolved by the LEX development team: the experimental item may be judged a good solution to the problem and merged into the item's main line of descent, or the development team may reject the integration team's fix and resolve the problem in a different way.

Consider what would happen if no experimental change procedure were available to the integration team for the ACOMP compiler. It is most likely that the integration team would make changes anyway, but in an uncontrolled way. As always, change control must provide well-defined, visible procedures that are appropriate to the task in hand.

9.8.4 Changes to baselines

A baseline is a fully approved product of a phase of the project lifecycle which forms the basis for subsequent phases. For example, a Software Requirements Specification (SRS) forms the basis for a Top Level Design Description (TLDD). A baseline may need to be changed during the development of a later baseline; for example, requirements may change or errors may be found.

The first rule of baseline control is that baselines must be kept up to date and accurate. If the TLDD cannot comply with the SRS, then the SRS must be changed. If the SRS is ignored by the designers writing the TLDD, then the SRS is hardly worth the paper it is written on; the SRS must be changed, and the change must be subject to the discipline of change control.

Many methods for developing software emphasise the importance of tracing the requirements defined by one baseline to their implementation in subsequent baselines. Thus a requirement in the SRS is satisfied by part of the design in the TLDD; this part of the TLDD in turn constitutes a requirement that is implemented by items of source code. The trace from a requirement to its implementation is a dependency of the implementation upon the requirement in the previous baseline. Figure 9.12 illustrates dependencies between items of successive baselines; these dependencies refine the crude dependency of the entire TLDD upon the entire SRS.

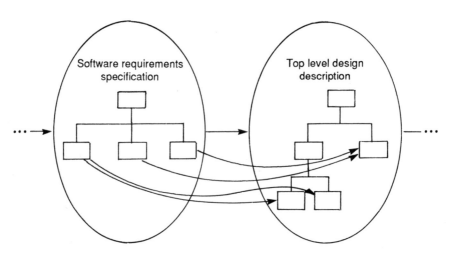

Figure 9.12   Dependencies between elements of successive baselines

The ability to trace requirements, or more generally to follow dependencies, is crucial if the CCB is to function effectively. Traceability between baselines is demanded by many software engineering standards, for example [DoD-2167A 88]. The impact of a proposed change to the SRS extends to those items of the TLDD which implement the item of the SRS that is to be changed. The CCB must take account of this impact when reviewing the CR. Note that the impact of a change to an approved baseline increases as the project progresses and more items in subsequent baselines become dependent upon the approved baseline. The CCB must also check that a proposed change to the TLDD continues to implement the requirements of the SRS.

Historically, change control has been largely concerned with changes to baselines. This chapter has emphasised a broader view of change control which encompasses changes to partially approved items, changes during software maintenance and dependencies between items which belong to the same baseline. Within this broader view, baseline change control remains an important aspect of CM.

9.8.5 Risk

It is not always possible to be sure of the full impact of a CR. There is then a risk that the change will have unexpected and undesired consequences. It is the role of the CCB to analyse this risk. The nature of the risk and the way it is analysed varies with the change. For example:

- The impact of a change to support software, whether developed or bought in, is often difficult to assess. The CCB may judge that it is too risky to upgrade to the latest version of a compiler just before the system is to be released to users.

- An item which is reused from another source, for example from another project within the same organisation, may be poorly understood and documented. A change to such an item may have unexpected consequences and is therefore risky.

- Any risk associated with a change to safety critical software endangers human life. The change control and risk analysis for safety critical software must therefore be formal and rigorous.

In each of these cases the CCB must analyse the risks associated with the change and weigh these risks against the benefits.

9.9 CONFIGURATION STATUS ACCOUNTING

One of the principles of CM is that it should be visible. *Configuration status accounting* provides this visibility by recording and reporting the status of all items and the status of all requests for change. Different people need different CM information at different times and in different forms. The questions which configuration status accounting must answer include:

- *What is the status of a item?* Many people will need to know the status of different items. A programmer will wish to know whether a specification has been fully approved and whether a subsystem which the programmer's code uses has been tested. The project manager will wish to track the progress of a project as items are developed and integrated.

• *Has a CR been approved or rejected by the CCB?* The originator of a CR will wish to know whether the CCB has approved the CR. For example, if a request for an enhancement to a library routine has been rejected as too expensive, then the originator of the CR must decide how to make do with the routine as it is.

• *Which version of an item implements an approved CR?* Once a requested enhancement to a library routine is implemented, the originator of the CR will wish to know which version of the routine includes the enhancement.

• *What is different about a new version of a system?* A new version of a software system should be accompanied by a document listing the changes from the previous version. The list should include both enhancements and fixes to faults. The information is part of the version description document (VDD) described in Chapter 5. Any faults which have not been fixed should also be described.

• *How many faults are detected each month and how many are fixed?* Faults are continuously detected during the operational use of a system; faults are also fixed by the team responsible for maintaining the system. Comparing the number of detected and fixed faults helps to assess the effectiveness of the maintenance team and to decide when a new release of the system should be made. It is also often useful to break down these statistics by priority of fault.

• *What is the cause of FRs?* FRs can be categorised by their cause. Categories of FR include, for example, violation of programming standards, inadequate user interface, inadequate performance and misunderstood user requirements. If a project manager knows that many faults have a similar cause, action can be taken to stop such faults recurring. For example, if many FRs arise because of misuse of global data areas then the project manager may restrict the use of global data.

The answers to these questions provide a record of progress and a record of change; they may be used by the project manager to monitor the progress of the project against the project plan and by the programmer to keep track of those changes which affect him or her. [Youll 90] describes many other uses of the raw data provided by configuration status accounting, and also describes how this data may be presented graphically to highlight different characteristics of a project.

This chapter has implicitly assumed a paper based approach to change control. Configuration status accounting is possible if CRs are held on paper—it just takes an inordinately long time to answer the sort of questions listed above. So long, indeed, that it may be thought not worth the effort! Projects which hold CRs on paper usually also maintain a *CR log* which provides an index to CRs. A CR log comprises a single line entry for each CR. Each entry contains basic information about the CR; at a minimum this should include the number of the CR, its status and the item to which it refers.

A CR log helps with some of the problems of paper based configuration status accounting. A better approach is for a CM tool to record information about both items and CRs in a database. The examples of configuration status accounting questions presented in this section illustrate how varied such questions can be. To cater for this variety, many CM tools provide a general purpose query language with which to make *ad hoc* queries about items and CRs.

CM tools for change control are the subject of the next chapter. Before leaving paper based approaches, it is as well to note that paper is rarely indispensable. It is unusual for everyone who may wish to raise a CR to have access to the CM tool. The usual solution to this problem is that a CR may be raised using a paper form; it is then passed to a change administrator who enters the CR into the CM tool.

Key Points

- Change control provides a visible procedure by which a change to an item is requested, evaluated, approved or rejected, scheduled and tracked.

- Every version of an item and every change request (CR) passes through a lifecycle. The nature of the lifecycle varies for different items and different CRs. Change control coordinates and controls these lifecycles.

- A paper CR form may be used to record the progress of a CR through its lifecycle.

- A fault report (FR) is a special type of CR which may merit a special type of form. An FR form should stress the circumstances and consequences of the fault, not the change which is needed to fix it.

- The change control board (CCB) is responsible for the integrity of items, for evaluating CRs and for the implementation of approved CRs. A large project may need several CCBs organised as a hierarchy.

- To be effective but not bureaucratic, change control must be sensitive to a range of factors. Deciding when and how to introduce formal change control is a project's single most important CM decision.

- Configuration status accounting reports the status of all items and all CRs; it provides a visible record of progress and of change.

10

TOOLS FOR CHANGE CONTROL

Change control is a management discipline which informs and controls the process of revising an item of software. In the last few decades, information technology has revolutionised the way information is managed. Paper documents, card indices and filing cabinets are things of the past in many areas of information processing. Information technology, in the form of CM tools, offers many benefits to the practice of change control. In view of these benefits it is, perhaps, surprising how many software projects continue to rely on manual methods. This chapter describes how CM tools can support change control. The principles are illustrated by descriptions of several widely used tools.

It is important to remember that no CM tool is a panacea for all CM problems. The purchase of a sophisticated CM tool is just one step towards effective CM. Using the wrong tool, or using the right tool ineptly or insensitively, makes CM problems worse not better. Later sections of this chapter describe how the use of a CM tool must be sensitive to the particular characteristics of each project.

10.1 HOW TECHNOLOGY CAN HELP

A CM tool can support the change control process in several ways:

- *Storing basic information about CRs.* The simplest change control tool is a database of CRs. When a CR is raised a new CR record is created in the database with the attributes discussed in Section 9.4; in particular, the record identifies the item for which a change is requested. The database is updated as CRs progress through their lifecycles. Section 9.9 noted the benefits to configuration status accounting of holding CRs in a database.

- *Support for impact analysis.* A tool for change control can hold information about items as well as CRs. It can also hold relationships between items such as when one item is part of, or depends upon, another item. The CCB must analyse the impact of a CR upon all items affected by the change. A tool can advise the CCB about which items depend upon the item to be changed.

- *Modelling the lifecycle of items and CRs.* Change control requires that an item is revised by performing certain activities which change the status of the CR (for example from raised to approved to implemented) and the status of a new version of the item (for example from under review to module tested to integration tested). A tool can monitor and control the interaction between the lifecycle of the item and the CR. For example, a tool can ensure that a new version of an item is not approved unless it implements an approved CR and can document within a source element the CRs which the element version implements.

- *Ensuring that the right people do the right thing at the right time.* The production of a version of an item requires different people to do different things at different times. For example, a user reports a fault, an engineer diagnoses the cause of the fault and proposes a fix, the CCB approves the fix and the engineer implements the fix, which is then approved by the quality manager on behalf of the CCB. A CM tool can ensure that these steps are performed in the correct order and that each step is performed by an authorised person.

- *Actively driving the process of change.* A CM tool can do more than passively check that a change control procedure is adhered to. It can drive that procedure by prompting the people involved to perform the next step and by informing interested parties of the progress of the change. Many tools make use of electronic mail for this purpose. For example, a tool may obtain the consent of everyone affected by a CR before the CR is approved, and may then notify these people when the change has been implemented and approved.

10.2 SIMPLE TOOLS FOR RECORDING CHANGE REQUESTS

Quite simple change control tools provide significant improvements to manual change control procedures. The tools described in this section are suitable for small to medium sized projects, up to roughly fifteen people, for which comparatively informal review mechanisms are adequate. They do not provide impact analysis or role modelling and are passive in the sense that they record change rather than drive it. Nevertheless, these simple tools help users, managers and engineers to communicate effectively, reliably and visibly.

10.2.1 Modification Request Control System (MRCS)

MRCS, described in [Knudsen 77], is an early example of a change control tool. MRCS is a sister CM tool to SCCS and Make; like these tools MRCS was developed at Bell Laboratories and is a component of the Unix Programmer's Workbench. The MRCS name for a change request is a modification request or MR. An MR form looks similar to the examples of CR and FR forms given in Chapter 9. The difference is that an MR is a form on a screen not on a piece of paper.

One of the design principles for MRCS was that it should be tailorable to the particular needs and working practices of different projects. Thus the data attributes associated with each MR, the validation criterion for these attributes and the way the attributes are layed out on the form can all be adjusted. Experience with general purpose change control tools since MRCS has supported this design principle: different projects have very different requirements for change control and these differences must be recognised by CM tools. Tools like SCCS and Make, which provide version and build control, are applicable to a wide range of projects. In contrast, change control tools are intimately bound up with the process of software development and the organisational structure in which this process is embedded. A change control tool must be adaptable to variations in this process.

Probably the most important variation between change control procedures is in the lifecycle of a change request. MRCS has no predefined lifecycle for an MR. An MR has a status which is implied by the next action which is required to progress the MR through its lifecycle. Each tailored variant of MRCS provides a set of permissible states for MRs. The validation criterion for the status attribute of the MR checks that the state transition implied by a change to this attribute is legitimate.

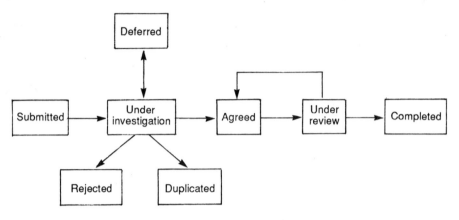

Figure 10.1   A typical lifecycle of an MR using MRCS

[Knudsen 77] describes an MR lifecycle which has proved useful in practice. Figure 10.1 summarises this lifecycle. An MR is entered into MRCS either directly by its originator or indirectly by a change administrator. The initial status of the MR is submitted. The change administrator makes an initial assessment of where the problem lies and designates the appropriate person to be responsible for investigating the MR; the status of the MR then changes to under investigation. The investigator fulfils the role of CCB for the MR by assessing the impact of the MR and then deciding what the next step should be. Of course the investigator may decide that he or she is the wrong person to review the MR, in which case the MR will be passed on to someone else, perhaps to a higher level of project management. When the investigation of the MR is complete, its status is changed to be one of:

- *Rejected.* The MR requires no further action; perhaps it arises from a misunderstanding or perhaps the proposed change is thought to be inappropriate.

- *Deferred.* The MR is deferred for a specified time, after which its status reverts to under investigation.

- *Duplicated.* If another MR requests the same change or reports the same fault, the status of the MR is set to duplicated and a reference is provided from this MR to the MR which it duplicates.

- *Agreed.* The requested change is accepted and becomes work in progress.

Once an agreed MR is implemented its status changes to under review. The new item versions generated by the MR are reviewed, both to check that they do indeed implement the MR and to confirm that the items have not regressed in any other respect. If the items fail this review then the status of the MR reverts to agreed and the items must be revised again. This lifecycle is a simple elaboration of the generic lifecycle described in Figure 9.4. It is suitable for medium sized projects where MRs can be investigated and implemented by one person.

A useful feature of MRCS is that it maintains an audit trail of every change to attributes of the MR. For example, the state attribute logs all previous states of the MR as well as the date at which the state transition occurred.

10.2.2 Change control using relational database technology

MRCS is built using the Unix technology of the 1970s. The database of MRs is held as a single 'flat' file. Configuration status accounting using this database is performed using a special purpose, stylised, limited function query language.

The 1990s offer relational databases with a general purpose query language (SQL) and facilities for developing form based applications. This technology makes it very simple to construct a change control tool like MRCS; further, the tool will enjoy a more ergonomic user interface, will be easier to tailor and will support multiple concurrent users.

All data held by MRCS may be held as attributes of one relation of change requests. Attributes of this relation record the item version to which the CR refers and the item version which implements the CR if it is approved. This very simple data model provides many of the benefits of automated change control, including flexible configuration status accounting using SQL. The model is easy to implement using most modern relational database management systems.

A more sophisticated approach would model entities other than just change requests, for example items and versions of items. The tool is then able to ensure that a CR refers to and is implemented by an existing item version. The data model may also capture relationships such as the dependency relationship between an item and the items which it depends upon and the component relationship between a composite item and its components. These relationships form the basis for impact analysis facilities of a change control tool. The reader should be cautious, however, before embarking upon the implementation of a sophisticated change control tool based on a elaborate data model. A simple change control tool is indeed easy to implement; on the other hand, the requirements and design for a tool which models items and their relationships are much more complicated and subtle. The rest of this chapter describes several approaches to the problems involved.

10.3 LIFESPAN

Lifespan is a general purpose CM tool which addresses all aspects of CM. The emphasis and strengths of Lifespan, however, lie in its methodical and rigorous approach to change control. Lifespan does not rival DSEE's facilities for defining and building configurations flexibly and efficiently. Lifespan provides automated support for controlling change and ensuring the quality of an evolving software system. Lifespan is a substantial advance on simple change control tools like MRCS in several areas:

- Whereas MRCS records information about items in the software library, Lifespan manages and directly controls access to the items. Only appropriately authorised Lifespan users have access to the software library.

- Lifespan ensures that any change to the software library is explicitly approved at two stages: when the change is proposed and when the change is implemented.

- MRCS has no knowledge of the structure of an item; an item to be changed is, from MRCS's perspective, atomic. Lifespan uses its knowledge of how items are aggregated to control the evolution of composite items.

- Lifespan models the dependencies between items. This relationship is a crucial input to the change control process; it enables Lifespan to determine which items are affected by a proposed change and therefore who must agree to the change.

- Lifespan uses electronic mail to drive change control actively. For example, affected parties must agree or veto a change within a certain time. If an affected party neglects to respond, the manager is informed!

Lifespan's approach to these and other change control issues is summarised below.

10.3.1 The package structure

The key relationship between Lifespan items is when one item *contains* another. Lifespan calls an item which contains other items a *package*. Of course a package can itself be contained in a higher level package. Furthermore, one item can be contained in several packages, so the package structure is not a strict hierarchy like the design item hierarchy described in Chapter 3. By convention, every Lifespan package contains itself.

Packages form the basis of control in Lifespan. Each item can only be checked out, modified, checked in and approved in the context of a package. An important example of the use of the package structure is that a proposed change to an item must be agreed in principle by the package manager responsible for each package which contains the item.

The contains relationship is between a version of a package and a version of each of the items the package contains. The version of a component item may either be identified explicitly, for example as version 1.3, or implicitly as the latest version in the software library. A package which contains a latest version component is mutable: when a new version of the component is checked into the library then the package containing it evolves. In Lifespan, every component of a package which is approved or under review must be explicitly identified, thereby ensuring that the package is frozen.

10.3.2 Updating the software library and design changes

The Lifespan software library is updated using the standard check out and check in model first described in Chapter 4. In Lifespan, any update to the library must be the subject of a *design change*, or *DC*. A DC is a very precise type of CR: it identifies exactly which items are to be changed as well as how they are to be changed. Lifespan software performance reports, described in Section 10.3.4, provide a separate mechanism for recording faults and enhancements where the cure for the fault or the changes required for the enhancement are not yet defined.

The complete lifecycle for a DC is described in Section 10.3.3. This section illustrates how a DC permits an update to the software library. Figure 10.2 shows the evolution of a fragment of a package structure. Version 1.3 is an approved version of a package M which contains version 2.2 of X and version 2.4 of Y; because the package M is approved, the versions of its components are explicitly identified.

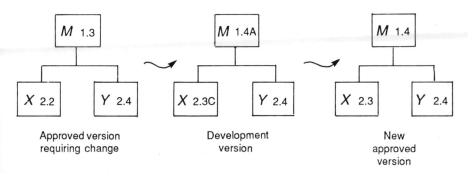

Figure 10.2   Updating the Lifespan package structure

To create a new version of *M* which contains a new version of *X* a design change must be agreed which describes the changes to these two items. New development versions of *M* and *X* may then be checked into the software library to create package structures like that illustrated in the second part of Figure 10.2. The alphabetic suffix to the version identifiers (1.4A and 2.3C) signal that these items are under development as part of a DC and are temporary. The contains relationship from version 1.4A of *M* to *X* specifies that the most recent version of *X* is to be used, in this case version 2.3C.

When the development of the package *M* is thought to be complete it is submitted for approval. At this moment Lifespan freezes the package so that no further versions can be checked in. If the package is approved then the alphabetic suffixes to the version identifiers of *M* and *X* are removed and the relationship from *M* to *X* is made explicit so that *M* contains version 2.3 of *X* rather than the latest version. If the package is not approved then it is unfrozen to allow development work to continue.

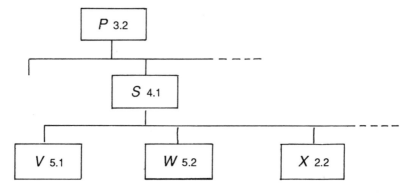

Figure 10.3   Other packages containing the mathematical routine *X*

Suppose now that *M* is a package of mathematical routines and that *X* is used by a subsystem *S* of a program *P*. Figure 10.3 shows the Lifespan package structure for the program *P*. The revision to the package *M* does not affect these items, even though the DC for the revision to *M* must have been approved in principle by the package manager of *S*. Version 4.1 of *S* still contains version 2.2 of *X*, not version 2.3 which is contained in version 1.4 of *M*. To upgrade *S* so that it uses the new version of *X* a second DC is needed. This DC allows the development of the new version of *S* shown in Figure 10.4. There is still no version of the program *P* which uses the new version of the mathematical routine *X*. A third DC is needed to develop version 3.3 of *P* which contains version 4.2 of *S* and therefore version 2.3 of *X*.

This approach to updating the Lifespan package structure is methodical and, perhaps, cumbersome. The revision to *X* has propagated in three steps

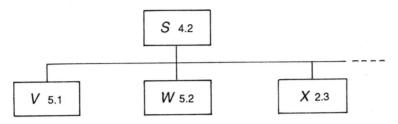

Figure 10.4 A new version of the subsystem *S*

from the mathematical library *M* to the subsystem *S* and thence up to the program *P*. There are other approaches which involve different DCs but achieve the same result:

- Several minor changes, such as that to *X*, may be collected together and presented as a rationalised upgrade. The upgrade would still follow the three step procedure described above.

- A single DC may be used for the updates to each of *X*, *M*, *S* and *P*. This approach might be used to fix an urgent and serious fault in *X*.

- *S* may be the subject of a DC which is unrelated to the change to *X*. The developer of *S* may then decide that the development version of *S* should contain the latest version of *X*. Until *S* is submitted for approval and frozen, new versions of *X* are used as they are checked into Lifespan.

10.3.3 The design change lifecycle

The lifecycle of a DC is illustrated in Figure 10.5. This lifecycle is the only way to revise an item; the lifecycle cannot be tailored and allows no shortcuts, for example, for an emergency change. There are three phases in the lifecycle of a DC: the objective of the first phase is to get the DC agreed by all interested parties, the DC is implemented during the second phase and is reviewed in the third phase.

When a DC is created it comprises a description of the proposed change, a list of the items to be changed and any additional information which documents or supports the request for change. The additional information should refer to related DCs or software performance reports (see Section 10.3.4).

Lifespan then determines the people affected by the DC. A Lifespan user is deemed to be affected by a DC if the user is the package manager for any of the packages to be changed or for any package which contains an item to

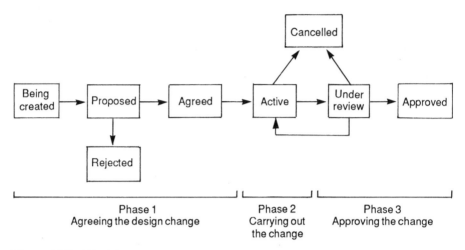

Figure 10.5   The lifecycle of a design change

be changed. The affected users constitute the CCB for the proposed change. Note that the manager of a package which contains a package that contains an item to be changed is deemed not to be affected by the DC. For example, the change to M and X of Figure 10.2 affects the package manager for S but not for P (see Figure 10.3). This algorithm limits the number of people who are required to agree to a DC. In particular, it ensures that not every DC escalates to the manager of the top level package, who will probably not understand the context of the proposed change. The algorithm is not perfect—the effect of some DCs will ripple more than one level up the package structure—but it is pragmatic and is consistent with the principle of information hiding.

Every affected user is then informed of the proposed DC by electronic mail and votes on whether the change should be implemented. If every user votes in favour of the change the DC is agreed. If one or more user votes against, then the DC is rejected. Typically, after a DC is rejected the affected users negotiate to produce a new DC which supersedes the one which has been rejected. If an affected user does not vote within a certain time the request is repeated and, if necessary, escalated up the organisational hierarchy of users maintained by Lifespan.

The next stage in the lifecycle of the DC is that it is taken up by a developer who will modify a package. The developer must be, or must become, the manager of this package, which must contain all the items cited by the DC. Often several related DCs are taken up at once, in which case the package must contain each item cited by each DC. It is often convenient to create a package specially for the change.

When a DC is taken up its status becomes active. The developer is able to check out and check in new versions of items cited by the DC as described in Section 10.3.2. Lifespan does not allow two DCs which cite a common item to be active at the same time unless each DC is taken up by the same developer for the same package. In the course of his or her work, the developer may find that items need to be revised which are not cited by the DCs that have been taken up; in this case another DC must be created, proposed, agreed and taken up by the developer.

When the developer believes that the work is finished the revised package is submitted for review. The package is then frozen so development versions can no longer be checked into Lifespan. A nominated and suitably qualified Lifespan user is now responsible for reviewing the package. The objectives and mechanism of the review are beyond the scope of the CM tool, but the review will often involve people other than the reviewer known to Lifespan. If the new version of the package is approved then:

- The package and its components acquire approved status.

- The package and its components are unlocked, thereby allowing another DC which cites them to be made active.

- The status of the DCs which are implemented by the new version of the package changes to approved.

- Affected users are notified by electronic mail that new item versions are available.

- Temporary versions of items which were checked into the software library during the course of the development can be deleted.

If the new version of the package is rejected by the review then its status reverts to active. The developer may then continue work on the DC to address the problems detected by the review.

The Lifespan review process can only approve one package at a time. Any contained package must already be approved before the higher level package is submitted for review. This rule ensures that a reviewer is not required to approve a large body of work at different levels of abstraction. A new version of an element is promoted to inclusion in successively higher level packages by a series of separate reviews.

10.3.4 Software performance reports and software status reports

Raising a Lifespan DC requires the change to have already been designed and thought through. All the items which need to be modified must be cited by the DC. Clearly a DC is not an appropriate mechanism for users of a software system, who probably know nothing of its internal structure, to submit a request for change.

Lifespan provides *Software Performance Reports,* or *SPRs,* for reporting a fault or for requesting an enhancement to a software system. An SPR identifies the versions of the items which it describes. The aim of this identification is to allow the report to be investigated, not to identify the items which need to be changed. Typically an SPR refers to high level items of the Lifespan package structure which are visible to the SPR's originator.

Software Status Reports, or *SSRs,* are used to report the current status of software managed by Lifespan to users of the software. In particular, SSRs are used to respond to SPRs. An SSR is not necessarily the last word on the subject of the SPR to which it responds. For example, an SSR may describe a temporary work around for a fault reported by an SPR; when the fault is fixed by a DC another SSR reports the fix and closes off the SPR.

SPRs and SSRs are the way in which the users of a software system and its developers communicate. Lifespan ensures that each SPR is the responsibility of a developer who is regularly prompted to respond to the SPR with an SSR until the SPR is closed. However, SPRs and SSRs are less formal documents than DCs and drive the process of change less directly.

Figure 10.6 summarises the relationships between the entities managed by Lifespan. This data model is the basis for Lifespan's configuration status accounting facilities. Entities, for example Lifespan users, and relationships which have not been discussed in this overview of Lifespan are not shown in Figure 10.6.

Lifespan's approach to change control is that SPRs are used to capture observations, suggestions, requests and faults in a system. SPRs lead to DCs which define precise changes to items. A case study in [OU 87] illustrates that this approach applies more widely than the change control of software.

10.3.5 Using Lifespan in practice

Lifespan's rules, especially those which dictate how a DC is agreed and a new version of a package is approved, guarantee that change control is tight, formal and secure. The rules cannot be circumvented nor can they be changed. This rigidity is both a strength and a weakness of Lifespan: a strength because it guarantees integrity; a weakness because it does not help a project to adopt a more flexible approach to change control. For example, when a Lifespan item is under development it is locked and cannot be changed as part of any other development. In practice there are several ways to ensure that Lifespan's change control methodology is not a bottleneck for

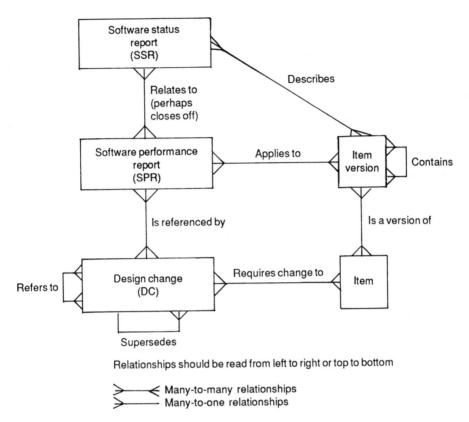

Figure 10.6   Entities and relationships managed by Lifespan

a project. One is to design the package structure carefully so that the number of people who need to agree a change request is not onerous. Another is to use less formal tools such as SCCS and Make to manage items while they are checked out of Lifespan. Outside Lifespan's control, SCCS may be used to branch the version tree (recall Figure 4.3) for the working version of a Lifespan item; the branch is merged before the item is checked back in to Lifespan. This approach ensures that variance is both temporary and localised. Lifespan meets the CM needs of managers by taking responsibility for items which have already achieved some degree of approval; SCCS and Make allow programmers to develop temporary variants and to build derived elements.

10.4 CHANGE AND CONFIGURATION CONTROL (CCC)

The CM tool CCC comes in two forms. CCC turnkeys are CM tools with similar scope and objectives to Lifespan. CCC native product provides the lower level facilities which are used to construct the turnkeys. A project using CCC either uses one of the turnkeys or uses the native product to construct a CM tool suitable for its particular needs.

One of the CCC turnkeys is called CCC/Development and Maintenance (CCC/DM). CCC/DM addresses most aspects of CM but, like Lifespan, the heart of the tool is its approach to change control. The description of CCC/DM which follows concentrates on this aspect of the tool, and contrasts it with Lifespan. Other CM issues addressed by CCC/DM, for example identification, variant configurations, configuration status accounting and building derived items, are not discussed in detail.

10.4.1 CCC/DM releases and configurations

The CCC/DM methodology for developing a sequence of *releases* (or baselines) is illustrated in Figure 10.7. Each release is held as four *configurations*: *development, test, approved* and *production*. Each configuration comprises the items of the release organised as a design hierarchy; CCC/DM does not constrain the depth or structure of the hierarchy.

As work proceeds on a release these configurations evolve in a methodical way: modified or new items are first checked into the development configuration; these items are then reviewed in the test configuration; items which

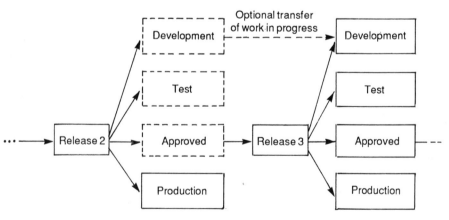

Figure 10.7   The CCC/DM release cycle

pass their review are collected in the approved configuration. The progress of an item through these three configurations corresponds to its approval status. The production configuration contains the versions of items which are in operational use outside the CCC environment; it can only be changed by following an emergency maintenance procedure which is outside the standard development and test cycle.

When the current CCC/DM release is *closed* all its configurations are frozen and a new release is created. A release may be closed for a variety of reasons; for example, the work planned for the release might be complete, or a periodic update to the production configuration might be due, or a snapshot of work in progress might be thought to be worth preserving as a potential fallback. Each configuration of the new release is initialised to be the same as the approved configuration of the release which has been closed. If there is any unapproved work in the closed release then this work can either be discarded or can be propagated to the new release; this is shown in Figure 10.7 as the optional transfer of work in progress. The old production configuration is archived in the CCC software library.

CCC/DM's configurations correspond to the use of operating system directories discussed in Chapter 6. In Figure 6.2 the DEV and APP directories correspond to the development and approved configurations of CCC/DM; the directories labelled 1.1, 1.2, etc., are snapshots of the APP directory and are analogous to the old production configurations held by CCC/DM. Although CCC/DM and the approach outlined in Chapter 6 have a similar basis, CCC/DM addresses many additional CM issues. For example, CCC makes economical use of disk space by storing similar configurations as deltas and CCC provides a change control procedure for updating configurations.

The Lifespan analogue of CCC/DM's development, test and approved configurations is the status of an item. A revision of a Lifespan item is first temporary, then under review and then approved. It is interesting to contrast the approaches of CCC/DM and Lifespan in this area. Suppose two items X and Y have each been independently revised, and that both of these changes have been tested and approved. In CCC/DM the development, test and approved configurations each contain the new revisions of X and Y; the production configuration contains the old revisions of X and Y until the release is closed. There is no configuration which has as components the old revision of X and the new revision of Y. By contrast, a Lifespan package containing both X and Y can be changed so that it contains the new revision of X, or of Y, or of both; any such change must be the subject of an explicit DC.

Lifespan packages are promoted through levels of approval; a package may be defined using arbitrary combinations of item versions subject only to the constraint that the approval level of a package cannot be higher than any of the items it contains. In CCC/DM, the level of approval of an item is defined by the configurations to which it belongs. The Lifespan approach is more formal; the CCC/DM approach is more pragmatic.

10.4.2 Change control

In CCC/DM one or more change requests (CRs) are implemented as a *project*. A project may be just one small change to one element or it may comprise all the changes required for the next release of the system. CCC/DM has no concept of item ownership analogous to the Lifespan package manager. Unless an item is under active change, it is not the responsibility of a specific CCC/DM user. CCC/DM provides four general roles, each with its own powers and responsibilities:

- *Configuration manager (CM)*. The CM is responsible for the configuration management of a system held by CCC/DM. The CM initiates all projects, assigns a project manager and test manager to each project and identifies the CRs which the project will implement. The CM is also responsible for closing the current release.

- *Project manager (PM)*. The PM is responsible for a project created by the CM. The PM nominates a developer for each CR of the project, identifies the items which will be changed as part of the CR and monitors the progress of the project.

- *Developer*. A developer is assigned to each CR. The developer checks items out of the CCC library, modifies the items cited by the CR and checks these items back into the development configuration of the current CCC/DM release.

- *Test manager (TM)*. The TM is responsible for testing changes made as part of a project. The TM tests and reviews items in the test configuration of the current CCC/DM release.

A CCC/DM user can be assigned to more than one of these roles. Also, a role can be assigned to more than one user so, for example, a small team may be made jointly responsible for implementing a CR. The central role of configuration manager can define assistants who have a subset of the CM's privileges. CCC/DM uses electronic mail to inform the users assigned to a role of relevant events in the progress of a project and its CRs.

Figure 10.8 summarises the lifecycle of a CR in CCC/DM. When a CR is created, it is assigned to a project by the CM. The CR moves to development status when the PM for the project identifies the items which need to be changed and nominates developers to perform these changes. While the CR has development status, the nominated developers check the items cited by

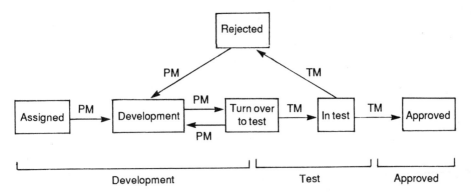

Figure 10.8   Summary of the lifecycle of a CR in CCC/DM

the CR in and out of the development configuration of the current release (steps 1 and 2 of Figure 10.9). When an item is checked out of CCC/DM it is locked, so it cannot be checked out to implement another CR. Unlike Lifespan, however, CCC/DM does not restrict the circumstances in which CRs which cite the same item can have development status at the same time.

When the development required by the CR is complete and all the items to be changed have been checked back into the library, the PM turns over the CR to test. This step automatically notifies the TM that the CR is ready for testing. There are two possible transitions from this state: either the CR is accepted for testing by the TM, or the PM may decide that further work is needed to complete the CR and return its status to development. If the CR is

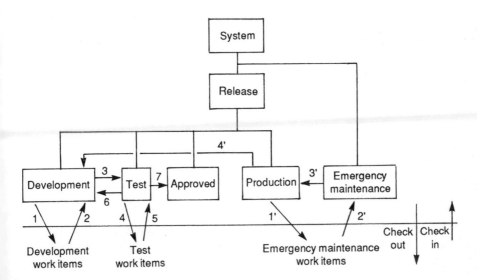

Figure 10.9   Changing and testing items in CCC/DM configurations

accepted for testing by the TM the items which have been changed as part of the CR are copied to the test configuration (step 3 of Figure 10.9). Items are then checked out of and in to the test configuration by the TM (steps 4 and 5 Figure 10.9). CCC/DM allows the TM to check in to the test configuration revisions to items which are cited by the CR but have not been changed by the developer. For example, the TM may need to modify the test code for an enhancement which has been implemented in the development configuration.

The TM then rejects or approves the CR: if the TM rejects it then the PM returns the CR to the developer for further work; if the TM approves it the changed items are promoted to the approved configuration (step 7 of Figure 10.9) and the CR is approved. Once approved, the CR can only be undone by raising another CR to reverse the changes.

Figure 10.10 shows the complete lifecycle for a CR in CCC/DM. It includes two states not shown by Figure 10.8: hold and deassigned. If the PM puts a CR on hold, no items may be revised to implement the CR; the PM reactivates the CR by changing its status to development. If a CR is deassigned the changes which have been made to implement the CR are deleted from the CCC/DM software library.

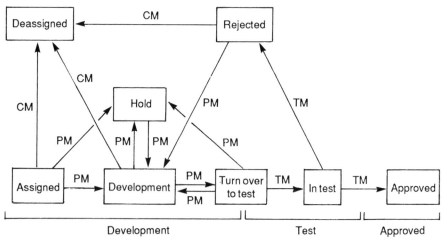

Figure 10.10   The complete lifecycle of a CR in CCC/DM

10.4.3 Emergency changes

The change procedure summarised above is the standard way to update the CCC/DM software library. Exceptionally a quicker procedure is needed to update the production configuration. Suppose a serious fault is found which has an obvious fix. Using the standard procedure this fix cannot be included in the production configuration until the release is closed.

Figure 10.9 illustrates CCC/DM's emergency change procedure for updating the production configuration. The first step is to define an emergency maintenance project which allows a developer to check items out of the production configuration (step 1' of Figure 10.9). When the emergency changes have been made the revised items are checked back into the *emergency maintenance configuration* (step 2' of Figure 10.9) which serves as a holding area for emergency changes. It is then the responsibility of the CM to decide whether the emergency change requires further development work, should be abandoned or should be included in the production configuration (step 3' of Figure 10.9).

If the emergency change is included in the production configuration then all development PMs working on items affected by the emergency change are notified by electronic mail; they must then decide whether to incorporate the emergency change.

Note that the emergency change procedure is outside the normal development and test cycle. In effect, the procedure creates a temporary variant configuration in the sense illustrated by Figure 4.3. There are two ways in which an emergency change may be merged into the approved configuration (step 4' of Figure 10.9) and thereby into the main line of descent. The first is that if the emergency change affects an active development project then the development PM is notified of the emergency change by electronic mail; the PM then has the option of incorporating the change as part of the project. The second is to create a development project to merge the emergency change into the main line of descent. If the emergency change is not merged into the approved configuration then it will not be included in the next CCC/DM release.

CCC/DM's emergency change procedure must be used very carefully! It must not degenerate into a shortcut for hard pressed developers to get their changes into production use without having to worry about change control. On the other hand emergency changes are sometimes needed. If CM does not provide a procedure for urgent changes, the project team will invent its own unofficial approach—and control will be lost.

10.4.4 Summary

CCC/DM provides a pragmatic but controlled approach to implementing agreed changes. To perform a change the configuration manager creates a project with a project manager who assigns developers to change items. This approach is flexible, but it places a lot of responsibility on the configuration and project manager.

CCC/DM does not support the process of deciding whether or not a proposed change should be implemented. There is nothing in CCC/DM which corresponds to Lifespan's impact analysis and subsequent voting by affected package managers; CCC/DM has no concept of item ownership. Projects which need tool support for CRs that have not been agreed can use CCC/DM in conjunction with a separate problem management tool which records fault reports and enhancement requests which may then lead to CCC/DM CRs.

The implementation of change using CCC/DM is a little less formal than using Lifespan. The description in this section has provided three examples of this:

- An item may be cited by several CRs which are under development at the same time in different contexts.

- Items may be checked in directly to the test configuration.

- The emergency change procedure for urgent changes to the production configuration.

This flexibility of CCC/DM can be extremely useful, but it also reduces the level of CM control. It is easy, however, to tighten CCC/DM's control of change by using native mode CCC to block any or all of these three facilities.

10.5 THE DIFFERENT REQUIREMENTS OF DIFFERENT PROJECTS

This chapter has summarised two sophisticated and widely used CM tools: Lifespan and CCC/DM. These tools each provide and support a particular approach to change control. Sometimes a project can adopt a turnkey change control tool like CCC/DM or Lifespan exactly as it is provided by its supplier; the facilities provided by the tool may match very closely the project's requirements or the project may use the tool to define its approach to change control. Often a project needs to adapt a change control tool before it can be adopted. Many attributes of the project affect the facilities which the tool should provide, for example the role of the CCB, the lifecycle of an item and of a CR, and the established working practices of the organisation undertaking the software project. As a general rule a change control tool should support the project's chosen change control procedures: the tool should meet the CM requirements of the project, not the other way round. Purchasing an expensive CM tool is not a magic answer to all of a project's CM problems. The tool must be chosen carefully, used intelligently and, often, adapted to the project's particular needs.

10.5.1 Tailoring change control tools

There are several aspects of a change control tool which may need to be adapted. This section summarises four of the most important areas.

The lifecycle for change

The change lifecycle may be short and simple; for example, a change may be first proposed and then either rejected or implemented. Alternatively, the lifecycle may be complex and may involve review, detailed design and impact analysis by different people in different roles. The project may wish to support only part of a complex change lifecycle with a CM tool, for example from the stage at which the change has been agreed. A tool which automates the early stages of the change lifecycle may need to differentiate between fault reports and enhancement requests and between CRs which originate from within the project team and from a customer.

The lifecycle of an item

The item lifecycle is closely related to the change lifecycle. It too may be simple and involve a single review, or it may be extended. Different types of items, such as documentation and code, may have different lifecycles. A CM tool may manage an item throughout its lifecycle, or it may only manage items which have already achieved some level of approval, perhaps because they have been developed elsewhere.

A project might choose to forbid or to allow concurrent development work on the same item. The restriction against concurrent development might be applied at the level of an element, or a subsystem, or even the complete system. Any concurrent development requires a mechanism for merging the temporary variants which result, be they DSEE elements or CCC configurations.

Configuration status accounting

A CM tool manages a database of information about items and CRs. Every transaction performed on the software library must be recorded in this database. The CM tool uses the information in the database to provide the configuration status accounts required by the project. Suppose that a particular status report is needed, for example

List the items which depend upon the items changed by CR number 27.

The CM tool must model the data referred to by the query (the items changed by a CR and the dependency relationship between items) and must present the report in the required format.

Integration

The CM tool should be integrated with other tools in the software engineering environment. The user interface of the CM tool should have a similar look and feel to other tools; the software library should be the single repository for all data which is used by all tools; all tools should be coordinated so that, for example, it is easy and natural to follow each step and use each tool involved in fixing a fault. The subject of tool integration is discussed further in Chapter 11.

10.5.2 Tailoring the lifecycle using PCMS

The previous section described areas in which it should be possible to tailor a change control tool to meet a project's particular requirements. There is a problem for tool suppliers here: the more flexible the CM tool, the more effort and expertise is needed to tailor the tool.

Product Configuration Management System (PCMS) [Montes 88] concentrates on providing flexibility for the lifecycles of items and CRs. A PCMS *control plan* defines these lifecycles. The control plan is defined to PCMS at the start of the project although it is possible to modify the control plan later, perhaps to add stricter controls. The key parts of a PCMS control plan are:

* *Roles.* The roles required to develop and maintain a project managed by PCMS and the names of the people who will perform those roles. Roles are associated with items in the PCMS item hierarchy. Some roles, for example project manager, will be performed by the same person for all items in the hierarchy. Other roles, for example developer, will be performed by different people for different items.

* *Lifecycles.* Each lifecycle is defined by a set of states and the roles which can change these states. Figure 10.11 shows a simple PCMS lifecycle which is suitable for a document.

- *Item types.* The types of item which will be managed by PCMS, for example documents, subsystems and elements of code. Each item type is assigned a lifecycle by the control plan; for example, the document item type might have the lifecycle shown in Figure 10.11.

- *CR type.* Typically the types of CR distinguish faults from enhancements and CRs which originate from clients and from within the project team. Each CR type has an associated lifecycle and template. The template defines the layout of the CR and the information it contains; it includes variables such as originator, priority and affected_items. Each instance of the CR replaces these variables with corresponding values held by PCMS.

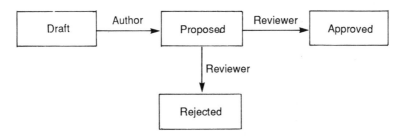

Figure 10.11   A simple PCMS lifecycle for a document

The lifecycle of an item version or CR defines the stages of its evolution. As an example consider a document with the lifecycle shown in Figure 10.11. When the document is created it has the initial state in its lifecycle: draft. In this state the item is mutable. It may be changed by the PCMS user who has the role of author for the document without creating a new revision. When the author completes the work PCMS is instructed to promote the item to the proposed status. PCMS then uses electronic mail to tell the reviewer that the document has been promoted and that it should now be approved or rejected.

PCMS only allows an item revision to be modified while it is in its initial state. For the lifecycle of Figure 10.11, to make a correction required by the reviewer a new revision of the document must be created. Figure 10.12 shows a more complex lifecycle for a document. With this lifecycle the reviewer has the option of returning a revision of a document to draft status for further work by its author; alternatively, the reviewer may reject the document and require the author to produce a new revision.

PCMS implements the lifecycle of a CR in a similar fashion. The role assignments for a CR lifecycle are derived from the role assignments for the

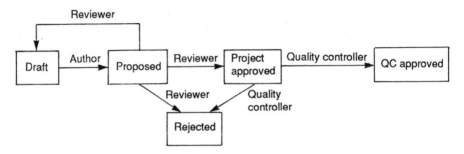

Figure 10.12   An extended PCMS lifecycle for a document

items affected by the CR. For example, the role of reviewer for a CR which changes a document is performed by the person who has the role of reviewer for the document.

Note that, unlike Lifespan and CCC/DM, PCMS does not restrict the implementer of a CR to change only the items cited by the CR. In particular, it does not require that a new revision of an item must be the subject of a CR. Instead PCMS relies on the people who approve items and CRs to ensure that the items have been revised in an appropriate way and that a CR has been satisfactorily implemented.

PCMS is a good example of a change control tool which can be tailored to meet a project's individual requirements. The lifecycle for a CR can be adapted to be consistent with an organisation's change control procedures and to model the roles which must be involved in the decision making processes. The complexity of lifecycles for items and CRs increases with the size of the project and the formality of its CM and quality control procedures.

Key Points

- Tools can assist with many of the mechanical aspects of change control, for example configuration status accounting.

- MRCS records basic information about CRs. Similar tools can be constructed quite easily with a relational database and fourth generation tool.

- More sophisticated tools for change control model the progress of items and CRs through their lifecycle and manage the evolving configurations.

- Lifespan provides strict and formal facilities for reviewing and implementing a design change (DC). Lifespan determines who is affected by a proposed change and requires their explicit approval before the change is implemented.

- CCC/DM provides a pragmatic approach to CM which is based upon four evolving configurations: development, test, approved and production.

- PCMS is an open CM tool which can be tailored to a project's particular requirements. The PCMS control plan models the structure and lifecycle of different types of item and CR.

11

MANAGING THE
SOFTWARE LIBRARY

The software library is the heart of software CM. It contains everything that is important to a software project: source code, user and system documentation, test data, support software, specifications, project plans and derived items.

This chapter discusses how the software library should be managed and highlights the central role of the library in the software engineering environment. The first section discusses the security and integrity of the library. Subsequent sections describe how the library is the linchpin which integrates all the software tools in the environment.

11.1 SECURITY AND INTEGRITY

11.1.1 Security and access control

The software library must be secure: it must only be accessed in ways which are consistent with sound CM. Both read access and write access must be controlled, the former to prevent unauthorised disclosure and the latter to prevent unauthorised change or deletion. Insecure access to the software library can arise in many ways:

- *Accidental corruption.* A careless engineer might type 'delete *.*' only to realise that the entire software library has accidentally been deleted from disk!

- *Malicious corruption.* Viruses, Trojan horses and logic bombs are unpleasant facts of life against which the software library must be protected. A client will not thank a supplier who delivers a system which has been infected by one of the supplier's mischievous employees; the client is more likely to call a lawyer.

- *Well-intentioned but misguided attempts to bypass CM controls.* An engineer may be convinced that a change is urgent or obvious or essential and that the normal change control procedures are not needed. All that is needed to make the change is to edit just one line of one file, and, if the version number is not changed, no one will ever know....

- *Fraudulent access and confidentiality violations.* The library may contain items which are commercially or militarily sensitive, or it may contain the result of millions of dollars of research and development. Access to such items, even if only for reading, must be rigorously controlled.

The type and rigour of access control which needs to be applied to the software library varies enormously between projects. If fraud and confidentiality are not issues, then a project may allow read access to all items in the library. There are, however, risks in making source code available to users who may then tamper with the code to create their own unsupported variants; a supplier may decide that such users need to be protected from themselves!

Some small projects use CM tools which do not protect the software library from unauthorised updates. Suppose a project uses the directory structure of Figure 6.3 to hold its software library. Each subsystem is assigned a design authority from the project team. Every change to a subsystem must be supervised and approved by its design authority. These procedures are well understood by everyone in the project team, but they are not enforced by automated access controls: anyone can check items in and out of any subsystem. This approach relies upon the professionalism and good intentions of the project team; it does little to avoid the four types of unauthorised access listed earlier.

A more secure approach is to protect the directories shown in Figure 6.3 using simple access controls. Many operating systems provide facilities which restrict who can read from and who can write to which directories. Using these facilities, the directory structure may be protected so that only the subsystem design authority can update the DEV directory, only the test manager can update the APP directory and no one can update frozen directories.

Some projects require items to be protected by strict and enforced access controls. [DoD 85], published by the US DoD and known as the Orange Book because of its bright orange cover, defines a framework for assessing the security controls provided by a software engineering environment. The Orange Book describes two types of access control:

- *Discretionary* access controls restrict access to an item based on the identity of the item and the access rights of the user. The control is discretionary in the sense that a user can pass on access rights to other users. The access controls outlined for the directories shown in Figure 6.3 are discretionary in this sense.

- *Mandatory* access controls restrict access to an item on the basis of the security classification of the item and the formal authorisation of the user to access classified items. For example, items could be classified as unrestricted, restricted, confidential, secret or top secret; a user might be authorised to access confidential (and therefore restricted and unrestricted) items, but not secret or top secret items. Mandatory access controls cannot be passed on from one user to another.

The Orange Book enables software engineering environments to be classified according to the extent to which they provide these two types of control. As yet there are few environments which are highly secure in Orange Book terms, although more are expected in the next few years.

Many CM tools provide access control facilities independently of the host operating system. For example, Lifespan places what amounts to a protecting wall around its library so that the library can only be accessed via the tool. Lifespan's wall is particularly impenetrable because it encrypts and decrypts items as they are checked in to and out of the library. Within the wall, Lifespan's access controls can be tightened by using passwords to protect individual items.

11.1.2 Integrity and backups

Data integrity requires that data is in some sense correct. Correctness is required both at the low physical level of bits and bytes, as well as at the high conceptual level which takes account of the meaning of the data.

CM tools are unable to ensure the high level integrity of the items they store: a tool cannot prove that a program is correct. At a lower level, items in the library may be required to meet certain syntactic quality criteria. For example, items of code should compile cleanly and should comply with the requirements of the project's quality plan, perhaps by having a header in a certain format. Some CM tools can be tailored to test these kinds of criteria whenever a new version of an item is checked in to the library; if the test fails the tool declines to accept the item.

At the lowest level, the CM tool must store items reliably. Engineers must be confident that any item checked into the library can subsequently be checked out. There are a range of practical techniques which reduce the risk and consequences of corruption of the software library:

- The security controls described in Section 11.1.1 should be used to protect the library from corruption by unauthorised access.

- All updates to the library should be part of a transaction. If something goes wrong during a transaction, for example a disk becomes full, then the transaction rolls back and the library reverts to its state when the transaction started.

- Any corruption of the library should be detected as soon as possible. Many CM tools include a utility which checks the integrity of the library; the utility should be run both regularly and after major updates.

Despite these precautions, corruption of the library is still possible. Hardware or software may fail, or the building containing the library may burn down! To cater for these risks, the library must be *backed up*, typically to a magnetic tape which is then stored in a safe place. If the library is corrupted, the project is able to recover the library from the backup tape.

A project must analyse carefully the risks of corruption to the library and determine its backup strategy accordingly. The library should be backed up sufficiently frequently that if it were corrupted then the cost to the project would be known and acceptable. This usually requires that the library is backed up at regular intervals, for example every day or week.

It is risky to rely on just one backup tape. How is the library to be recovered if corruption is not immediately detected and the backup is also corrupt? What happens if the library is corrupted while the backup tape is being written? It is good and common practice to cycle round a set of two or more tapes, using each in turn to hold a backup.

A library backup may be full or incremental. An incremental backup contains only that part of the library which has changed since the previous backup. To save time and space a project might take a full backup every Monday night on tape A and an incremental backup on other working days on tapes B, C, D, etc. If the disk is corrupted on Thursday, the project can recover the library as it was on Wednesday night by first restoring the full backup from tape A and then applying the increments on tapes B and C.

11.1.3 Archives

Given infinite disk capacity, all versions of all items would be stored in the library in perpetuity. In practice, available disk space is limited. Even if the library uses a delta storage mechanism, it is often necessary to conserve disk space by deleting items and by archiving items to secondary store such as magnetic tape.

An *archive* differs from a backup in several ways:

- An archive does not replicate data in the software library; it holds data which is no longer in the library.

- Archives are usually written irregularly and are kept indefinitely; backups of the library are usually written at regular intervals and kept for a limited time.

- An archive usually holds one version of an item from the library, for example a fully approved baseline. A backup is usually a snapshot of the library and may contain several versions of one item.

There are several rules and guidelines for when items should be deleted from the library and when archived. One rule is that software which has been released to a client may be archived but should never be deleted. Another rule is that an item must not be deleted unless all items which depend upon it can also be deleted.

As a guideline, if there is a later revision of an item which has achieved a higher level of approval then the old revision is a candidate for deletion. Another guideline is to keep the most recent two or three revisions of an item at each level of approval. Figure 11.1 illustrates these guidelines applied to a succession of item revisions. The figure is a snapshot at the time the latest revision is checked into the library. The height of the vertical line above each revision is a measure of its approval status.

A project's archive strategy should be based upon the expected need for historic item versions. As with backup strategy, it is better to be safe than sorry.

11.2 RELEASE MANAGEMENT

From time to time software is issued or released from the library to users of the system. Figure 11.2 illustrates how this differs from checking an item out of the library to create a new version.

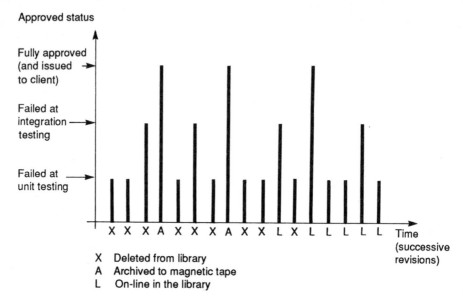

Figure 11.1   Deleting and archiving old revisions from the software library

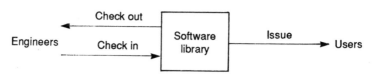

Figure 11.2   Issues from the software library

11.2.1 Producing the release

Software released to a client or to users must comprise items which have been approved as fit for their intended use. Usually this requires that the items are fully approved by the CCB, although beta test or prototype releases may be less than fully approved. It also requires that the correct variant of the system is issued to the client. The payroll system described in Chapter 4 has variants for different operating system platforms and for different countries; a French client with a Unix workstation will not be pleased to receive an English version of the payroll system for VMS.

It is rare for a client to be issued with a version of every item in the design hierarchy. For example, clients of the payroll system should not be supplied with source code or system documentation. Release procedures must identify precisely which items the client requires. This is best achieved by maintaining, as an item which is itself controlled and approved, a list of items to be included or excluded from a release. This list then automatically determines which items are issued to the client.

11.2.2 Release notes

A release to a client must identify itself by the version, i.e. revision and variant, of the top level item in the design hierarchy from which its items are drawn. It should also include release notes which describe:

- Demands which the system makes upon its environment. For example, the payroll system running on a PC may require a maths coprocessor and OS/2 at version 3 or greater.

- How to read the magnetic media, install the system and then run tests which verify that the system has been installed correctly.

- How to upgrade from an earlier version of the system. For example, the database maintained by the payroll system may need to be modified in some way before it can be used with the new release.

- A list of the known faults and limitations of this version of the system.

- A summary of the differences between this and previous releases of the system, for example a list of faults fixed and enhancements made.

- How the client should communicate with the supplier to report faults, request enhancements and obtain help with problems.

The detailed content of release notes varies enormously. The above list is an indication of the sort of information which should be provided with a release. Release notes must be managed as an item like any other. They are often the first part of the system which the client sees, and first impressions can be important.

11.3 TOOL INTEGRATION

CM is not, of course, the only discipline which is needed to develop and maintain software. Methods and tools are also needed for design, project planning, software testing and a host of other activities. All these activities overlap and all depend upon CM: each has an end product or deliverable which must, sooner or later, be subject to CM controls.

To be effective, all the tools in the software engineering environment must be integrated. The ultimate aim of tool integration is that the boundaries between tools should be seamless; the environment should be perceived by its users as a single tool which has been designed as a whole. This section discusses three dimensions for tool integration and summarises frameworks for describing and structuring an integrated environment.

11.3.1 Integration dimensions

A seamless software engineering environment must be integrated in three dimensions: the user interface of its tools, the data shared between these tools and the way in which simple tools cooperate to perform complex tasks.

User interface

To achieve user interface integration, all the tools in the environment must have a similar look and feel. In an environment which is not integrated, some tools have a WIMP (window icon mouse pointer) interface while others have a menu or command driven interface. Of the tools which use a mouse as an input device, some use only one mouse button and some use three. The tools using three mouse buttons use different buttons to mean 'select'; different tools interpret select in different ways.

It is not sufficient that all tools use, for example, X windows; that is just the first step. The interface of each tool must use the same conceptual model, for example the desk top metaphor of the Apple Macintosh or the control panel metaphor described in [Sommerville 89], and must use this model in the same way. Deep integration of the user interface is very hard to achieve. The benefits it brings in ease of use and in productivity can be enormous, as is exemplified by the Apple Macintosh environment.

Data

Tools in the environment often need to share data. For example, a project management tool and a CM tool might both hold information about workpackages, items and release dates. Data integration requires that data used by different tools is shared effectively. There are two approaches to data sharing. The simpler approach is that tools pass data between each other as and when they need to. To support this approach, the CDIF (CASE Data Interchange Format) standard defines a format for exchanging data between CASE tools. The more powerful and ambitious approach to data integration is that all data is held in one place which is accessed directly, subject to appropriate controls, by all the tools in the environment. Several names are used for this shared datastore, for example repository, data dictionary, encyclopaedia, object management system, library or engineering database. Following IBM's lead and influence this book uses the word repository.

It is not sufficient that all tools use the repository, they must have a common understanding of the structure and meaning of the data. This common understanding may either be defined in some way by the repository or agreed between cooperating tools. For example, the IRDS (Information Resource Dictionary Systems) standard [Goldfine 85] defines the meaning and structure of the repository data, whereas a simple operating system file store imposes little structure and less meaning on the data it holds.

Control

Software engineering tasks require that the right people do the right things with the right tools in the right order. For example, to revise an element of code it must be checked out of the library, an editor invoked, and changes made and tested before the element is checked back into the library. With control integration the environment coordinates the use of individual tools, not the engineer. Control integration allows the engineer to work more reliably, more quickly and without knowledge of the operation of individual tools.

The Unix operating system provides some basic but effective mechanisms for coordinating simple tools; these mechanisms include command files (or shell scripts in Unix terminology) and a way of 'piping' a stream of data from one tool to another. To achieve control integration, the Unix philosophy must be extended to more sophisticated tools and to more complex, and less procedural, task descriptions.

11.3.2 Integration frameworks

The *onion* model illustrated in Figure 11.3 has often been used to describe the structure of an Integrated Project Support Environment (IPSE). The core of the onion is the host operating system upon which is built the repository layer which holds data shared by the tools in the next layer. Tools communicate

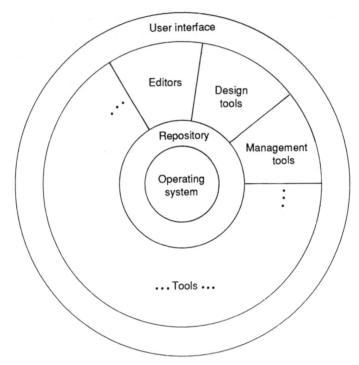

Figure 11.3   The onion model for an integrated project support environment

with users through the outermost layer of the onion which provides the basis of user interface integration. If the environment is open, then tools may be added to it using the Public Tools Interface (PTI) to the repository and the user interface.

There are other similar models of the structure of the software engineering environment. Figure 11.4 illustrates the ECMA (European Computer Manufacturers Association) reference model for CASE environments; tools slot into this framework like pieces of toast in a toaster. The reference model extends the onion model by making control integration an explicit part of the model.

The reference model provides a common language for discussing integration frameworks. Thus, for the Unix environment, shell scripts are task management services in the reference model and pipes are part of the message server network. Some integration frameworks, for example that proposed by the IBM AD/Cycle [IBM 89], provide coverage for all areas of the reference model; others, for example Unix, only address some areas of the model.

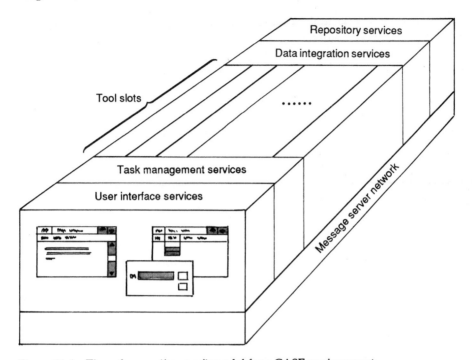

Figure 11.4   The reference ('toaster') model for a CASE environment

11.4 INTEGRATION AND CM

From the perspective of CM the important dimensions of integration are data and, to a lesser extent, control. CM tools manage a library of items which are produced by other tools in the environment. It is a principle of CM that all the data that is important to a project must be configuration managed. The repository therefore equates to the software library, and tool integration requires that all tools, including CM tools, share repository data in a controlled way. This section reviews some of the issues involved in integrating a CM tool with other tools in the environment.

11.4.1 The granularity problem

A major practical problem for data integration is that many CASE tools do not provide items which a CM tool can configuration manage effectively. The general case of this problem is sometimes called the granularity problem.

It arises when one tool produces coarse grained data which is used by another tool, but the first tool hides the data's fine grained structure.

Consider DFDdraw, an interactive tool which maintains a set of related dataflow diagrams (DFDs) that describe the design of a system. DFDdraw stores all its diagrams in one monolithic file, the internal structure of which is known only to the tool itself. DFDdraw ensures that, within this file, all the diagrams in the set are consistent. DFDdraw is a fictitious tool, but the problems it illustrates are far from imaginary.

The problem with DFDdraw is that, from the perspective of a CM tool, it constrains all the dataflow diagrams in the design to be a single element. This may be acceptable if the design produced by DFDdraw is produced by one engineer and if there is only one variant of the design. For a large design, it is likely that parts of the design which are represented by individual diagrams need to evolve separately. CM is then a serious problem: there is no way to identify versions of parts of the design, configurations cannot be built from different versions of different diagrams and it is hard for two designers to work independently on different diagrams. The data which DFDdraw provides is too coarse grained for effective CM.

One approach to this problem is for DFDdraw to enable parts of the design to be exported as operating system files and subsequently reimported. Alternatively, DFDdraw may store each diagram in the set as a separate operating system file. Either way, the tool provides fine grained data which can be configuration managed. These kinds of mechanisms are useful but sometimes lead to practical difficulties. DFDdraw must also be able to combine different versions of individual diagrams to form versions of the complete diagram set. This may require delicate reconciliation between the diagrams if the interfaces are not carefully defined. Interfaces between fragments of data managed by CASE tools are rarely as well defined as the interfaces between elements of code.

Some CASE tools recognise the importance of CM and take on responsibility for it themselves. For example, DFDdraw might store multiple versions of each dataflow diagram in a set and might provide facilities for defining and building configurations of diagrams and for change control. The trouble with this approach is that it is closed and therefore precludes data integration. After a system has been designed using DFDdraw it must be coded and tested, perhaps in Pascal. A different CM tool must be used to manage the Pascal code. Worse, this tool will not know about the dependency of an element of Pascal code upon the dataflow diagram which specifies it. Traceability between design and implementation has been lost.

The granularity problem is very real and very important. It arises when one tool ignores the existence of other tools in the software engineering environment. The solution is effective data sharing. A tool must produce data fragments which are small enough to be CM elements; if it does not, its place in the environment must be questioned.

11.4.2 Distribution

The distribution of the software engineering environment is often a serious obstacle to data integration. If a development or maintenance project is distributed between several sites how can data be shared? The ideal solution is to use a networked filestore to hide geographical distribution. The software library may be physically distributed between several nodes of a network, but this distribution is transparent to library users. Among the tools described in this book, DSEE provides best support for distribution in this sense. The nodes of the DSEE network illustrated by Figure 7.3 may be in different offices or buildings.

Unfortunately, it is rare that the problems of distribution can be solved this easily. A more usual scenario is that a large project is divided into several subprojects, each of which uses a different software engineering environment. For example, one subproject might use Unix to develop part of the system while another subproject develops Ada code using the Rational Environment; specifications and design documents for the system might be written using a word processor on a PC. In this scenario the distribution is heterogeneous not homogeneous: different parts of the project are using different methods and tools.

The problems posed by heterogeneously distributed projects are among the most difficult for CM. What constitutes the software library for such a project? How and where are configurations defined and built? How are items moved between different sites? One approach to these questions is that items of low approval status are managed, developed and built locally, but as items are approved they are promoted to central CM control. This approach is illustrated in Figure 11.5. The central CM system might be administered by a prime contractor who is responsible for integrating the software produced by the three subprojects, or it might be the responsibility of the integration and test team in a single organisation. The emphasis of the central CM system is on the more formal, management aspects of CM such as change control and security; it must accept items which have been developed or derived by subprojects and, viewed from the central system, may have an incomplete change or derivation history. Conversely, the CM emphasis for the three subprojects of Figure 11.5 is to allow programmers to define and build configurations easily and flexibly.

Sometimes practical problems arise when items are moved to the central CM system. For example, word processor documents produced on a PC

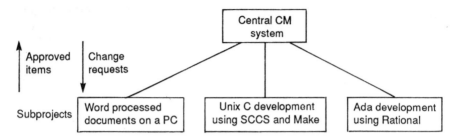

Figure 11.5   An example of heterogeneous distributed CM

may be meaningless in the environment of the central system; to examine a document it must be transferred back to the PC. It is, of course, essential that there is no loss or corruption of data when items are transferred to and from the central CM system. Control characters embedded in the element and information about the structure of the file containing the element (its record length, block size, end of record markers, etc.) must all be preserved.

It is not always possible for all items to be held by a central CM tool. Clearly hardware items cannot be held by a software tool! Sometimes it is not practical to transfer all software items to a central library on a central machine. In these cases it is useful for the central CM system to record the existence of an item, even though it does not actually store the item itself. Many CM tools support the concept of a *remote item* for which the software library contains a pointer to the item instead of the item itself. A CM tool can do part of its job for remote items, for example it can record its version history and CRs against the item, but enforced controls are lost.

11.4.3 Beyond the check in and check out model

The model for CM used in this book assumes that all items are held in a software library; engineers check items in to and out of the library as they are needed. This is a good, practical approach but it has two limitations: firstly, most CM tools do not tackle the issue of control integration; secondly, CM tools wash their hands of items while they are checked out of the library. These two limitations are related. A more integrated approach to CM never loses sight of items but is integrated seamlessly with the revision process.

Suppose a developer needs to modify an element of code to fix a fault. With an integrated approach to CM, the developer points the editor at the element and starts making changes. Transient, working revisions of the element are all captured by the CM tool, but have a very low approval status. At times chosen by the developer the CM tool saves a revision at a higher approval status. The tool keeps an old revision at the explicit request of the developer, but otherwise discards old revisions following the guidelines outlined in Section 11.1. When the engineer compiles the element of code, the object code generated by the compiler is automatically captured by the CM tool which records the relationship between the derived element and revision of the source element from which it was derived. When the fix is believed to be complete the engineer requests that the status of the element is promoted to be under review. Providing the element passes certain quality checks, for example that it compiles, then the request is honoured. The status of the derived object code is automatically inherited from the status of its source.

With this integrated approach, the CM tool never loses sight of an item—even when it is being developed by a programmer; there is no concept of a developer's private work area which is beyond the scope of the CM tool. The integrated approach to CM contrasts with the classical approach which regards the software library as a secure but remote safe in which engineers store their code when it has been approved. Among the tools described in this book, DSEE and Rational Environment come closest to being integrated in this sense.

11.5 THE REPOSITORY: REQUIREMENTS, IMPLEMENTATIONS AND TRENDS

All of the CM tools described in this book store elements as operating system files. Usually these files are protected so that they can only be accessed by the CM tool (see Section 11.1.1). Many tools store successive revisions as deltas (see Section 4.5). Different tools use different approaches for storing information about items and the relationships between them: some, such as PCMS, use a general purpose relational database; many others use their own private and special purpose database.

The models for integration frameworks described in Section 11.3.2 suggest a different approach: the CM tool should use the repository to store items and information about items. For this approach to work the repository must provide the services needed by CM tools. This section summarises the particular requirements of CM tools and how these requirements are addressed by different repositories.

All the other sections of this book describe practical methods and tools for CM. This section discusses repositories which are not, at the time of writing, in widespread use. It is clear, however, that the day of the repository is fast approaching and that the impact of the repository on CM methods and tools will be enormous.

11.5.1 Requirements for a repository

Any database management system, whether it contains company accounts, cartographic data or repository data, must provide basic functions such as security, integrity and concurrent access by multiple users. In many other areas a repository has particular requirements which distinguish it from the database of a typical commercial information system. The most important requirements for a repository are listed below.

- *Complex structures.* A composite item such as a subsystem has a complex substructure. Sometimes the item should be managed as if it had no substructure, for example to query the version number of the subsystem; at other times the fine grained structure of the item must be visible, for example to revise one of its components. The repository must allow complex structures to be assembled and then manipulated as a whole.

- *Versions.* Updates to a commercial database are usually destructive. For example, changing a person's telephone number in a telephone directory database overwrites the old number. Conversely, a change to an item is frequently represented as a new revision; each item in the repository has many versions which have both significant similarities and significant differences. The repository must provide mechanisms for identifying, creating and managing versions of items and for storing multiple versions efficiently.

- *Variable length data.* All databases store data values which, from the perspective of the database system, have no internal structure and are indivisible. In a relational database, a data value is called an attribute; usually it is short and has fixed length. In a repository, data values may be very long, for example an executable program, or very short, for example a single type declaration or information about an item such as its version number. A repository must be capable of storing long data values, but it must also store short data values efficiently. If it is inefficient to store many small items then the repository encourages tools to store coarse grained data, and thereby incites the granularity problem described in Section 11.4.1.

- *Nested transactions.* [Date 90] defines a transaction as a logical unit of work. A transaction serves as both a unit of locking (two transactions cannot update the same data at the same time) and as a unit of integrity (if the transaction aborts then the database is unchanged). For a commercial database, a transaction, for example to transfer money from one account to another, usually takes a matter of seconds. It is less clear what constitutes a transaction for a repository. Is fixing a fault one transaction? Or building a configuration? Certainly repository transactions last longer than most transactions on a commercial database. Further, in the same way that a complex structure contains components, a long transaction may comprise many subtransactions.

- *Views.* A view is a particular perception of part of a database. For a relational database, a view is defined using the relational algebra operations select, project and join. The most useful views of a repository usually contain one version of a subset of its items. The DSEE thread language described in Section 7.4 is a good example of a language for defining views of repository data. Views of a repository are needed to allow developers to work independently, to allow changes to be made without affecting other developers and to allow developers to refresh their view of the repository by including changes made in the context of another view.

- *Complex rules and triggers.* A database has rules which ensure the integrity of the data it contains and triggers which are activated when the database is updated in specific ways. For a commercial database, simple rules such as referential integrity are very powerful. For repository data, the rules are more complex and have wider scope. The repository should not be passive; it should make active responses to change. For example, when a new version of an item is checked into the library, affected users should be notified; they should not need to check periodically whether part of the repository has been updated.

Note that all of these requirements apply to any database which describes an evolving design, not just to a repository holding items. The design of an aircraft or a microprocessor or a software system all involve multiple versions, complex structures, nested transactions and sophisticated integrity rules.

An interesting and controversial question is the extent to which the requirements for a repository are compatible with the relational model. It is clear that some of these requirements make particular demands upon the way in which the relational model is implemented. One example of this is the requirement for variable length attributes; another is that a repository is likely to contain many different data types but few instances of each type, whereas a commercial database usually contains many instances of a few data types. Furthermore, the relational model provides no direct support for complex structures or versions; the model must be extended to include these facilities.

These observations do not imply that the requirements for a repository are incompatible with the relational model, or even that a repository cannot be built on top of a relational database. Experience with relational databases has shown the value of a high level, non-navigational query language like SQL and of the principle of data independence (separating the way in which data is viewed from the way it is structured and stored). Alternatives to the relational model ignore these and other lessons at their peril. See Chapter 25 of [Date 90] for an incisive discussion of this issue.

11.5.2 Portable Common Tools Environment (PCTE)

PCTE defines a platform which can be used to implement a software engineering environment. In terms of the reference model of Figure 11.4, PCTE provides repository and data integration services. The following brief description concentrates on those aspects of PCTE which are of value to a CM tool.

The PCTE *Object Management System (OMS)* stores *objects* which are connected by *links*. For example, an object which contains an element of source code might be linked to an object which contains the element derived from the source code by compiling it. Different types of link have different properties. Thus an object which is the destination of a link with the *referential integrity* property cannot be deleted, whereas the destination of a link with the *stability* property cannot even be updated. The link from a source element to a derived element usually has the stability property. The type of link also defines whether an object can be the source of more than one link of that type and whether two links of that type can have the same object as their destination. See [PCTE 88] for a complete description of PCTE link types and their properties.

Both objects and links have *attributes*, for example the approval status of an item would be an attribute of the corresponding PCTE object. Tool writers specify the data structures to be used by their tools as PCTE schema. The following is an example of PCTE schema.

```
c_function: subtype of element
   with
   attribute
      function_name: string
      tested: boolean:=false
   link
      specified_by: link to specification_document
      includes: link to include_file
      derives_to: link to object_module
end c_function
```

This example defines one object type called c_function which has two attributes and is connected by links to three other object types. The types of the links and the objects to which they connect are not shown in this schema fragment. The first line of the schema declares c_function to be a subtype of element. The types of PCTE objects form a hierarchy in which each object type inherits attributes and links from its parent types. An object type may be a subtype of more than one object type, in which case it inherits from each of its parents. Object types do not have associated operations, so PCTE is not really object oriented in the same way as programming languages like Smalltalk or C++.

One way in which PCTE addresses the needs of CM is by modelling composite objects. A *composite object* is defined by a root object which is connected by a set of *composition links* to its component objects which may themselves be composite. Formally, a composite object is the transitive closure of all the composition links from the root object.

A composition link type may be defined to be *exclusive*. An object can be the destination of only one exclusive composition link, so exclusive composition links enforce a strict hierarchy of objects corresponding to the design item hierarchy described in Chapter 3. Composition links which are not exclusive allow two composite objects to share components; in CM terms this corresponds to overlapping configurations. For many purposes PCTE allows a composite object to be manipulated in the same way as an object without components. For example, PCTE provides operations which copy, move, delete and lock an object and all the objects which are connected to it by composition links.

PCTE also provides mechanisms for managing versions of an object, which may of course be composite. The *revise* operation applied to an object A creates a copy of A to which it is connected by predecessor and successor

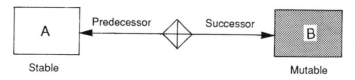

Figure 11.6   Versions of a PCTE object

links, as shown in Figure 11.6. The predecessor link type has the stability property so A, the destination of the link, is frozen. This models the CM principle that only the working version of an item is mutable. A new object can also be created by taking a snapshot. Applying the snapshot operation to an object B creates a copy of B, a successor link from the copy to B and a predecessor link from B to the copy. The way in which PCTE physically stores versions of an object is hidden from the PCTE user, however, economical implementations of PCTE hold successive versions of both composite and atomic objects as deltas.

The snapshot and revise operations may be used to define a version graph such as the one shown in Figure 4.3. A sequence of revisions is created by repeatedly revising or taking snapshots of an object; a branch line of descent to hold a variant is created by revising an object which already has a successor; a branch can be merged with the main line of descent by explicitly creating a successor link. PCTE ensures that the version graph has no cycles, so that an object cannot be one of its own successors.

PCTE also provides mandatory and discretionary access controls in the sense discussed in Section 11.1.1, as well as support for nested transactions. See [PCTE 88] for details of these facilities.

11.5.3 Information Resource Dictionary System (IRDS) and beyond

PCTE was designed as a platform for engineers using a third generation programming language such as Ada or C, often to develop a real time embedded system. The other computing community, that of commercial data processing and information systems, has also recognised the importance of the repository concept. This section discusses the most important initiatives towards a repository standard for this community.

IRDS was approved by ANSI, the American National Standards Institute, in 1989. See [Goldfine 85] for a technical overview of IRDS. Although IRDS originated as a standard for data dictionaries, its objectives and design are quite similar to those of PCTE. There are, however, some areas tackled by IRDS which are beyond the scope of PCTE. Two are described briefly below:

- *The IRD schema.* IRDS defines particular types of objects, relationships and attributes which tool writers will wish to store in the repository. The object types defined by IRDS include data objects like document, file and record as well as process objects like system, program and module. The idea is that all CASE tools need to store this kind of data in the repository and that the IRDS should define its structure so that CASE tools can share data. The problem is that it turns out to be very difficult to generalise and predict the data dictionary requirements of CASE tools. PCTE relies on tool builders agreeing between themselves the data structures which will be held in the repository.

- *The IRD lifecycle.* IRDS provides a simple model for the software development lifecycle. An organisation using IRDS defines a set of lifecycle phases, for example specification, high level design, etc. There are three types of phase: one *controlled* phase, one *archived* phase and many *uncontrolled* phases. Uncontrolled phases contain items which are not operational, for example specifications, designs and work in progress. The controlled phase contains items which are in operational use; it is modified by promotion from an uncontrolled phase. The archived phase contains obsolete versions of items. IRDS provides integrity rules and customisation facilities which define how an item progresses between lifecycle phases.

At the time of writing repository standards are in a state of flux. There are several technical developments and commercial considerations which will influence what happens next:

- *The draft ISO IRDS standard.* ISO (International Standards Organisation) IRDS is based upon ANSI IRDS but there are significant differences. The ISO standard is based squarely upon the relational model and SQL, unlike PCTE and ANSI IRDS, which may loosely be described as using an entity relationship model. Like PCTE, the ISO standard makes no attempt to predefine object types such as document, file and record; types must be defined by the IRDS user. ISO IRDS also introduces the concept of a working set which is a new and interesting way of modelling configurations.

- *ATIS.* ATIS (A Tool Integration Standard) is a proposal for the next version of the IRDS standard. It attempts to draw together the best of

IRDS (both ANSI and draft ISO) and PCTE. In ATIS the description of an object type includes its behavioural properties. Different object types exhibit different behaviour. For example, an element of Ada code is compiled with an Ada compiler and C code is compiled with a C compiler, whereas a document cannot be compiled. Attributes are inherited in the PCTE object type hierarchy; in the ATIS hierarchy behaviour is also inherited. ATIS also offers more support than PCTE and IRDS for the check out and check in model for revising items.

- *The IBM repository.* IBM's long awaited repository which is the heart of its AD/Cycle will soon be fact not fantasy. Each tool using the repository has its own conceptual view of repository data. For example, a CM tool and a project management tool perceive the repository in different ways. Each view has an associated set of policies covering security, integrity, derivation and triggers. Like ANSI IRDS, the IBM repository defines an 'information model' for repository data which enables tools to share data meaningfully; again like ANSI IRDS, IBM and IBM's business partners are finding it very difficult to define the structure of the information model. The repository is built on top of IBM's flagship relational database DB2 and has both an object oriented and an entity relationship interface. In short, the IBM repository has many exciting and ambitious features, but how it will all work in practice is not yet clear.

Key Points

- The security of the software library must be protected from unauthorised access.

- The software library must be regularly backed up as insurance against its corruption.

- Items which are no longer needed in the software library may be archived or deleted.

- The release of a software system to a client must be accompanied by comprehensive release notes.

- The software engineering environment contains many tools which must be integrated with CM tools. There are three dimensions of integration: user interface, data and control.

- Issues which CM integration must address include the granularity problem, distribution and the integration of the CM tool with the process of revising an item.

- The requirements of a repository differ from those of a database for a conventional information system. PCTE, IRDS (ANSI and ISO), ATIS and the IBM repository are examples of attempts to meet these requirements.

12

PLANNING AND ORGANISING SOFTWARE CONFIGURATION MANAGEMENT

Earlier chapters describe in some detail all aspects of CM: how items are identified, how versions are managed and how changes to items are controlled. This last chapter brings these threads together. It summarises how to go about CM in practice. It suggests when to do what, it highlights common pitfalls and proposes remedial action if things go wrong.

If software projects were all the same, then they could all perform CM in the same way. Unfortunately, or perhaps fortunately, every software project is unique, and this diversity is becoming broader with the introduction of new lifecycles, methods and tools. This chapter is therefore closer to a checklist than a cookbook.

12.1 THE CM PLAN

The CM plan is the document which describes how a project will manage configurations. It defines the who, what and when of CM. The CM plan may be part of the project's quality plan or, if the project and its CM plan is large and complex, it may be a stand-alone document.

The structure for a CM plan which is described below follows very closely the IEEE standard format [IEEE-828 90]. There are other ways of structuring the CM plan which provide the same information; however, the IEEE format is becoming widely accepted and provides a standard by which CM plans may be assessed.

1 INTRODUCTION

The introduction is an overview of the CM plan. It summarises:

- The scope of the plan by identifying the project, the software and lifecycle phases to which it applies.

- The purpose of the plan: the CM risks and objectives which are particular to this project and the approach to CM which they demand.

- The assumptions made and resources required by the plan, for example people, tools and client participation in CM.

- The relationship between the plan and other standards or plans which describe how the project is managed.

2 MANAGEMENT

The management section describes the organisational units which are concerned with CM and their responsibilities. Each CM activity which is described in Section 3 of the plan is assigned to one of these units. For a small project the units might be the client, quality assurance, a project manager and a configuration manager; for a large project the units might include subcontractors and a hierarchy of CCBs. The plan provides the terms of reference of each organisational unit which has CM responsibilities, in particular the unit's purpose, membership, authority and operational procedures.

3 ACTIVITIES

This section describes the activities to be performed by the organisational units described in Section 2.

3.1 Configuration identification

This subsection describes three aspects of configuration identification: which items are to be managed, how each item version is uniquely identified and how items are stored.

3.1.1 *Identifying items*

The plan describes the software which is subject to CM. It is neither necessary nor practical for the plan to list explicitly every item (although the project must maintain a list of items as they are produced). The plan identifies:

- The lifecycle phases and the baseline produced by each phase.

- The types of items in each baseline. For example, the plan might describe the structure of an element during the coding and testing phase as an Ada package, test data, a screen layout definition or a derived element.

- The levels in the design item hierarchy for each baseline. For example, the specification phase might have just one level of decomposition whereas the coding and testing phase might comprise subsystems and elements.

Where particular items are known, then they may be identified by the plan. For example, the plan may identify project standards and software tools which must themselves be managed. However, it is not the job of the CM plan to predict the structure of items which are not yet designed.

3.1.2 *Item names and versions*

The plan specifies how items and versions of items are uniquely identified. Items which are developed by third parties may need special consideration.

3.1.3 *Storing Items*

The plan specifies how items are stored in the software library and how the library is managed. This includes access and integrity controls, archive and backup procedures, and the physical labelling and storage procedures for magnetic media. If the library is distributed between several sites or machines then the plan must describe which items are held in which library and how each library is managed.

3.2 Configuration control

This subsection describes the procedures by which a change is requested, evaluated, approved or rejected, and implemented. It describes how this lifecycle varies with the baseline affected by the change, the impact of the change, the origin of the request for change and whether the change corrects a fault or is an enhancement.

3.2.1 *Requesting change*

The plan describes how a CR is submitted and the information which accompanies each request. This information must include the item to be changed, the originator's name and location, the date and urgency of the request and a description of the change and why it is needed.

3.2.2 *Evaluating change*

The plan describes how the impact of a change is assessed and quantified.

3.2.3 *Approving or rejecting change*

The plan identifies the CCB, whether an individual or a group, which approves or rejects a CR. If there is a hierarchy of CCBs, the plan describes the procedure which ensures that a CR is considered by the appropriate CCB.

3.2.4 *Implementing change*

The plan describes the procedure for implementing an approved change and the information that is recorded for each implemented change. This description includes:

- The lifecycle of all items and how an item is approved at each stage of its lifecycle.

- How configurations of items are defined and built.

- The procedure for building and delivering a release of the system.

- Any procedures for handing over the system to a different team, for example from a development team to a maintenance team.

3.3 Configuration status accounting

This subsection describes what information about items and CRs is recorded and how that information is made available to interested parties, for example by weekly reports to the project manager or by querying an on-line database.

3.4 Configuration audits

A configuration audit verifies that an actual item has the characteristics required by its specification. This section describes when configuration audits occur, what is audited, by whom and how any problems detected by the audit are resolved. At a minimum, there should be an audit at the end of each project phase and before a configuration is released to a client.

3.5 Interface control

Interface items define the interaction between the system and its environment. In general, a system has interfaces with its support software, with other systems and with its users. The cost of inadequate control of the items that describe these interfaces can be particularly high. This section identifies interface items and describes how they are controlled.

3.6 Subcontractor and supplier control

This subsection specifies how externally supplied items are managed. It describes:

- The items supplied, for example whether source code and development tools are included.

- The requirements for CM by the supplier, including the production of a CM plan, and how the supplier is monitored for compliance with these requirements.

- How supplied items are received, reviewed and merged with the project software.

- How changes to supplied items are agreed and implemented.

4 CM SCHEDULES

The CM activities described in Section 3 of the plan occur at different times. Some activities are constant throughout the project, some occur at particular times, others evolve during the project. The CM schedules section describes the sequence and coordination of all CM activities.

The most important schedule is that which describes the introduction of change control. The time at which an item becomes subject to a certain level of change control usually corresponds to it achieving some level of approval in its lifecycle, for example when the item is checked into the software library, or is approved in isolation, or is part of a configuration which has been audited. It is crucial that the schedule for change control is neither too onerous nor too lax.

5 CM RESOURCES

The CM resources section describes the resources which are needed to perform the activities described in Section 3 of the plan. Software tools, staff, training and equipment requirements are all identified.

6 CM PLAN MAINTENANCE

The CM plan maintenance section states who is responsible for ensuring that the plan is implemented, reviewed at regular intervals and changed when appropriate. Like all other items, the plan is itself subject to change control.

12.2 KEY FACTORS FOR CM PLANNING

[IEEE-1042 87] provides extensive guidelines for how to write a CM plan and gives four example plans. This section highlights seven key factors of which the CM plan must take account.

- *The size of the project.* The single most important factor which affects CM is the size of the project. For a project of three people, all CM controls can be exercised by the project manager. A project of thirty people needs a CCB and a configuration manager. A project of three hundred people will need a hierarchy of CCBs and a team of people responsible for managing the software library.

- *Project distribution.* A large project may be divided into several parts, each of which requires a different approach to CM. For example, each might use different CM tools or might develop different kinds of items. Even if each part of the project is similar, it may be difficult to communicate between the parts of the project; for example, it may be difficult for an engineer to access items developed by another part.
  For a distributed project, the plan must describe:

  - Effective CM procedures for each part of the distributed project.

  - How the interfaces between the parts are defined and controlled.

  - How configurations of the complete system are defined and built.

- *Dependence on third party software.* Almost all projects make some use of software supplied by third parties, if only a compiler and operating system. Some projects buy in substantial, bespoke items which will form part of the delivered software. Such projects must plan carefully how the third party software is to be specified, delivered, accepted and changed.

  Is the CM of the supplier organisation adequate? How and precisely what is to be delivered? Will the supplier or the purchaser maintain the software? If the purchaser, are the necessary resources available (source code, expertise etc.)? If the supplier, how are changes agreed and what happens if the supplier goes out of business?

- *The item types.* The types of items being developed and maintained can have a major practical impact on CM. Text documents, diagrams, compiled code, interpreted code and derived element tools all have different physical characteristics which affect how they should be identified, stored in the software library and used to define and build configurations.

- *The project phase.* Most of the factors which affect CM change during the project. For example, the first phase of the project might be to specify the system requirements. The number of people developing this specification is small, change control can be informal and tools are not needed to define and build configurations. By the coding and testing phase the project has grown. Communication among the project team must be formalised and changes to the specification and design documents produced by earlier phases must be carefully controlled. The plan must describe how CM evolves during the project lifecycle as new items are developed and the need for control of existing items increases.

- *One or many clients.* Many CM activities are simpler if the software system has only one client using one version of the system. If, however, like the payroll system described in Chapter 4, the system has many clients and must run in several environments then the CM plan must describe how:

  - Permanent variants of the system are managed.

  - Releases of the system to different clients are built and recorded.

  - Old versions of the system which are still in operational use are maintained, and for how long.

- *Management constraints on the CM plan.* The CM plan must recognise the constraints which affect how the project will be managed. It is unusual for the author of the plan to start with a blank sheet of paper; usually the CM plan must comply with imposed or established working methods. It may be necessary to comply with standards imposed from outside the project, for example by the client or by the larger organisation of which the project is a part. The plan must always take realistic account of the project's resources, including the skills and background of the project team.

  The CM plan is closely related to other management plans such as the project plan and the quality plan. For example, the quality plan will describe the conduct of formal reviews which control the progress of an item through its lifecycle. The CM plan must be consistent with related plans; where possible it should reference them rather than reiterate them.

12.3 ORGANISATIONAL STRUCTURES

12.3.1 Case study

Figure 12.1 is an organogram of a medium sized project of roughly fifteen engineers. The figure, and the discussion which follows, highlights those organisational units with specific CM responsibilities; of course these units have other responsibilities unrelated to CM. Although the case study is based upon a particular project, the principles it illustrates apply generally.

The *project board* is responsible for the project's overall objectives and for allocating the resources needed to achieve those objectives. It has three members: an executive who chairs the project board, the project manager and

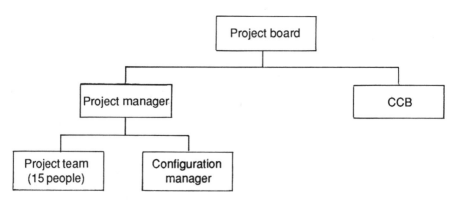

Figure 12.1   Case study organogram for CM

a senior client representative. The board must review and approve all project plans, including the CM plan.

The *project manager* is responsible for ensuring that the software system is produced on time, within budget and to the project's quality standards. Actual or anticipated deviation from the project's plans must be brought to the attention of the project board as soon as possible. The project manager submits the CM plan to the project board for approval and then ensures that it is implemented.

The *project team* designs and implements the software system under the direction of the project manager. The team must comply with all the requirements of the CM plan. CRs are implemented by the team at the instruction of the project manager (who is, in turn, directed by the CCB). Any member of the project team can originate a CR.

The *configuration manager*'s first task is to write the CM plan in collaboration with the project manager and is then responsible for implementing the routine aspects of the plan and for monitoring its day-to-day operation. In particular, the configuration manager:

- Initialises the required CM library structure to support the item identification scheme required by the CM plan.

- Ensures the security and integrity of the software library by implementing access controls and performing archives and backups.

- Implements the procedures to create new items and check items out of and in to the library.

- Provides configuration status accounts as they are needed.

- Informs interested parties when a change is implemented.

- Manages releases of the system to its clients.

Note that CM tools help the configuration manager to perform all of these tasks more reliably, effectively and quickly.

The CCB is responsible for the integrity of software produced by the project. It has three members: the project manager, a client representative and a quality assurance coordinator. When necessary the CCB is advised by engineers from the project team and is provided with status accounts by the configuration manager. The CCB approves or rejects CRs to approved items and monitors the implementation of CRs which it approves. If the impact of a CR exceeds certain defined limits then the CR must, in addition, be approved by the project board; in this way the project board acts as the top level CCB for the project.

12.3.2 The handover to maintenance

The CM plans and organisation discussed so far have largely addressed the needs of the development phases of a project. An important moment in the project lifecycle is when the system is first released to the client. For some projects this is the end of the lifecycle because responsibility for maintaining the system passes to the client. Other projects are responsible for maintenance of the system after release to the client but undertake no further development.

The most difficult case to manage is when the project must simultaneously maintain the system and make major enhancements to it, as illustrated in Figure 12.2 The version control aspects of parallel development and maintenance are discussed in the case study of Chapter 7. For all but the smallest projects it is common and good practice to divide the project team into two: a development team and a maintenance team. Without this division there is a risk that maintenance activities such as responding to urgent client fault reports will swamp development work. The maintenance team is sometimes called the support or production team.

The maintenance and development teams need different skills. The maintenance team usually has close contact with the system's users and it must be able to relate to their needs and concerns. It often includes staff who have themselves used similar systems. Members of the development team must be able to design and implement substantial new items of software; they usually have a more technical outlook and probably do not wear a suit to work.

Before the system is handed over to the maintenance team the project manager must ensure that the system is maintainable and that the team has the skills and resources it needs. The maintenance team must have a broad understanding of the system as a whole. When detailed knowledge of a part of the system is needed, for example to fix a fault, this must be available from system documentation. The team must be able to define and build configurations of the system, including old releases which must still be maintained and variants required by different clients. It is also crucial that the maintenance team has and uses regression tests to check that their changes have no adverse side effects.

During parallel development and maintenance it is the job of the CCB to decide when and how an approved CR should be implemented. If the change is needed urgently and can be made with the resources available to the maintenance team then it will be included in the next maintenance release. Otherwise the change will be made by the development team and included in the next major release. There are several advantages in assigning a change to the development team. It may be possible to include the change as part of a major enhancement to part of the system, perhaps one which supersedes the CR. Also maintenance changes constitute temporary variants which must be merged with development work before the next major release;

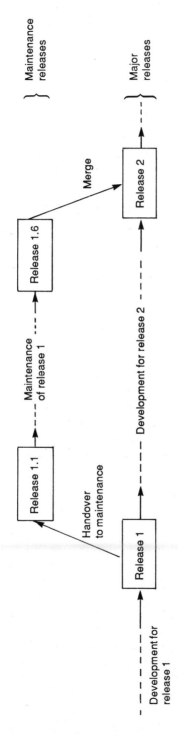

Figure 12.2   Parallel development and maintenance

Chapter 5 described the difficulties and risks of such merges. The CCB must weigh these factors against the urgency of the change. Although the CR may indicate the originator's perception of its urgency, the final decision rests with the CCB.

12.4 RESOURCING CM

CM is not an option for a software project. Recall the list of CM questions from Chapter 1. These questions arise for every project, and every project makes some sort of attempt to answer them. Not every attempt is methodical or effective.

What is the cost of inadequate CM? Imagine a project in which the items have no version identification and are modified directly so that the old state of the item is destroyed, in which a disk failure results in the irretrievable loss of all items, in which there is no control of change, in which there is no record of how derived elements are built and in which there is no control of when the system is released to its users. It is impossible to quantify the costs of this chaos.

It takes time and skill to plan, implement and monitor CM. In the case study of Section 12.3 there is one configuration manager for a project team of fifteen engineers. The project manager and members of the review board also spend a significant proportion of their time on CM. For a larger project the effort needed to provide effective CM depends significantly on how CM tools are used. [Boehm 81] estimates that between 5 and 10% of a project's effort needs to be directed towards CM and quality assurance, and that this percentage does not vary greatly with the size of the project. If the project does not make effective use of CM tools, then Boehm's estimate is probably low.

12.5 CHOOSING CM TOOLS

There are two rules to remember before embarking upon a survey of CM tools. The first rule is that different projects have different CM requirements. The first step in choosing a CM tool should not be to survey exhaustively the available tools; it should be to review why a tool is needed. Any other approach is analogous to designing a software system before it is specified. A CM tool may be needed for many reasons: it may be needed to provide management controls for approved items or it may be needed to help programmers in their day-to-day work of revising, building and testing software.

The second rule is that no CM tool is a panacea. A tool can address some CM problems but not all. For example, it cannot plan what level of CM controls are needed and when they should be imposed, it cannot judge whether a change is desirable and it cannot assign engineers to CM roles. Getting the best out of a CM tool is often more difficult than setting up a crude manual CM system. To present a project team with a gift wrapped CM tool accompanied by the words 'There, that's how you do your CM' is to invite disaster.

The following checklist of capabilities highlights the most important functions of a CM tool. For each question in the list, decide whether the tool's capability meets the requirements of the project for which it is intended; if the answer is no, then assess the importance of this deficiency.

A checklist of CM tool capabilities

Item identification

How are items named and how are versions of items identified?
Are items structured in a hierarchy?
What is the depth of the hierarchy? What information is held about each item and each item version?
Is an element's identity and derivation manifest as part of the element?

Version control

Does the tool use the check in and check out model? With locking?
Are versions of elements and composite items held as deltas?
Can temporary variants be defined, i.e. branches in the version tree?
Is assistance provided for merging temporary variants?
How are permanent variants modelled and supported?

Defining configurations

How is the structure of system described?
Does the tool separate the system model and version selection?
What criteria may be used to select item versions for a configuration?
Do the criteria include status, revision date and explicit version?
Is one developer able to choose when to adopt items revised by another?

Building configurations

Does the tool control how derived elements are built?
Are configurations built using existing derived elements whenever possible?

Is there a transparent algorithm for caching frequently used derived elements?
Is parallel processing used to assemble large configurations?

Change control

What lifecycles does the tool provide for items and change requests?
Can these lifecycles be modified and extended?
What information is recorded for each change request? Can this be tailored?
Must every change to an approved item implement an approved change request?
Are there facilities for grouping related change requests?
Does CCB membership for a change request vary with the item to be changed?

Configuration status accounting

What reports describe items, change requests and their relationships?
Is the database open so that *ad hoc* queries can be made, for example in SQL?
Can the tool report the differences between similar items?
Does the tool keep account of which configurations have been released to whom?

Integration and ergonomics

What is the user interface of the CM tool?
Is the tool well integrated (control, data, user interface) with other tools?
Is there a procedural interface to the library?
Is electronic mail used to inform and prompt the users of the tool?

Library management

Can the library hold all types of operating system file?
What access control facilities are provided?
Are there selective and incremental backup and recovery facilities?
How does the tool ensure and monitor the integrity of the library?
Can historic items be archived and restored?
Can the library be distributed? Between heterogeneous sites?
Can the library store items that have been derived outside its control?

Non-functional considerations

On which operating system platforms is the tool available?
Does the tool need any other software, for example a proprietary database?
How much does the tool cost?

Is the tool well documented and supported?
Is training and consultancy in using the tool available?

12.6 INTRODUCING CM TO A PROJECT

In [Bersoff 79], Bersoff *et al.* write of CM, 'Pay now, or pay later'. The point is
that if a project is not adequately configuration managed a day of reckoning
will inevitably ensue. Sooner or later, after missed deadlines, poor quality
releases and budget over-spends, someone, somewhere, will recognise that
the project needs CM. The phrase 'Pay now, or pay later' was once an
advertising slogan for automobile oil filters; if you don't invest in an oil
filter, or in CM, then dealing with the breakdown which ensues will cost you
dearly. Perhaps the slogan should be 'Pay now, or pay a lot more later'.

Unfortunately projects sometimes postpone thinking about CM until
things get so bad that the problems cannot be ignored. Wayward projects
often seek to solve their CM problems by hiring an expert consultant. There
is some sense in this: the project team may be so close to, and used to, their
problems that they cannot see the need for change, let alone how to change.
Whoever is charged with introducing effective CM to a wayward project has
a demanding job ahead. The following are some of the keys to success:

- Whoever leads the introduction of CM must be an expert in the subject,
  not a theoretician but a practitioner. At the very least he or she must have
  worked within well-managed projects of similar size and complexity.
  Ideally, he or she should have experience of resolving CM problems.

- If a sophisticated CM tool is to be used, then the CM expert should have
  used the tool before; here again theoretical knowledge is not adequate.
  If the CM expert has not used the tool, then help will be needed from
  someone who has, perhaps a consultant provided by the tool supplier.

- The CM expert must believe in the importance of CM and must be
  committed to its successful introduction. External consultants sometimes
  lack this commitment. As Ould notes in [Ould 90], every new method
  or tool needs a 'champion' to drive it through—someone who will not
  give up at the first hurdle but will adapt the method and tool to the
  needs of the project.

- The project team must support the introduction of CM. The team must
  be persuaded that CM is part and parcel of professional software
  engineering and that a little discipline will, in fact, make their job easier.
  This is usually quite easy to achieve if approached in the right way. Do

not, for example, proclaim that 'No one can change released code without filling in one of these forms' without at the same time explaining why.

- The aim of whoever introduces CM is to improve the way in which the project is managed. Once these improvements have been agreed they must be backed up by the authority of the project's management; ultimately CM procedures need more than goodwill to ensure their success. The project's management must also provide adequate resources to introduce CM, for example for training and tools.

- Do not attempt to change the world overnight. Try to introduce CM methods and tools gradually and to minimise disruption. On the other hand, avoid duplicating existing procedures; there is nothing more frustrating than having to fill in two forms with similar information to achieve one objective.

- If the project is in total chaos, the first priority should be to establish the library of items and to ensure the security and integrity of the library. Next, simple change control procedures should be introduced, especially for critical items such as those which define interfaces between subsystems. Restructuring items to exploit all the facilities of a sophisticated CM tool is a low priority: first get the items under the basic control of the tool and then restructure.

12.7 CONFIGURATION MANAGEMENT STANDARDS

Quality standards regulate both the process of software development and the product of that process. Coding standards which define how a programming language should be used is an example of a product standard. A CM plan is an example of a process standard. The requirement to comply with a standard can arise from several sources, for example an organisation's quality assurance department, the client for the software product or even from the law of the land. In each case, the purpose of the requirement is to improve software quality.

Standards come from many sources and have very different levels of generality. Public domain standards such as ISO 9001 make quite general requirements. These requirements are met by the more specific standards which form part of an organisation's quality management system. A project produces a quality plan which specialises the organisation's quality management system. Finally, individual workpackages are performed in a way

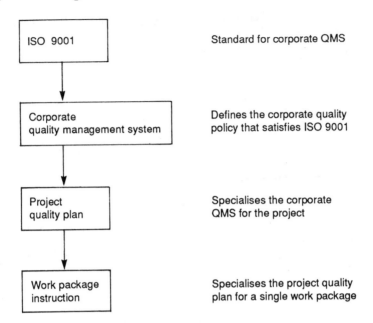

Figure 12.3   Specialisation in the hierarchy of standards

which is consistent with the project quality plan. This hierarchy of standards is illustrated in Figure 12.3 which is derived from a similar figure in [Ould 90].

The specialisation of a general standard to a more concrete standard which is appropriate to the context is crucial. As an extreme example, it is not helpful to require a programmer to write a Pascal program in accordance with ISO 9001!

This section describes standards which are in the public domain and which address CM. See [Hall 89] for a review of all public domain standards which are relevant to software development.

12.7.1 ISO 9001

ISO 9001 [ISO-9001 87] is an important general standard for 'design/ development, production, installation and servicing'. It is identical to the UK Standard BS 5750 and the proposed European Standard EN 29000. As illustrated in Figure 12.3, it imposes requirements for the standards which form an organisation's quality management system. Software suppliers are increasingly required by their clients to comply with this standard.

ISO 9001 is not specific to software. Its requirements apply to any industry which supplies a product. It is not always obvious how these requirements are to be interpreted for software. In the United Kingdom this interpretation is provided by [QAS 87]. Many of the twenty paragraphs of ISO 9001 are concerned, at least in part, with CM—evidence perhaps of the importance of CM in software development and maintenance! The most important CM requirements of ISO 9001 are summarised briefly below.

- *The software which must be managed.* Several paragraphs of ISO 9001 define things which must be subject to CM. These include the contract with the client, project plans and procedures, the design of the system, purchased software, the system itself as well as all software tools and development facilities.

- *Change control.* A change control procedure is required for all items. These procedures must provide for contract changes, design changes and service (i.e. maintenance) changes. In general a visible procedure must be provided to request, review and implement a change. The changes which implement a CR must be traceable from the CR.

- *Item identification.* All items must be identified by their name and version. The test status of all items must be recorded. Dependencies between items must be recorded to provide traceability of derivation. All items must be stored securely and reliably.

- *Purchased software.* The purchaser must assure that the supplied software has itself been developed using effective CM procedures, for example by ensuring that the subcontractor's quality system itself complies with ISO 9001.

- *Release management.* The release of items to clients must be documented and controlled. Procedures must ensure that only items which have been approved as fit for purpose are released.

12.7.2 Other public domain CM standards

The IEEE Standard for Software Configuration Management Plans [IEEE-828 90] was summarised in Section 12.2. It, and its associated guide [IEEE-1042 87], are the best public domain standards for software CM. It is compatible with ISO 9001 in the sense that a CM plan which complies with [IEEE-828 90] must address the issues required by ISO 9001.

Armed forces are major procurers of large, complex systems and use extensive sets of quality standards to regulate their suppliers, the defence contractors. Several of these standards address CM (see [Hall 89] for details).

Unfortunately, these standards are intended at least as much for the CM of hardware as of software and are therefore difficult to interpret for software. They are not recommended either as bedtime reading or for guidance in software CM.

Finally it is worth noting that standards which are not primarily concerned with CM are increasingly including requirements on how software configurations are managed. For example, the interim UK standard for safety critical software requires sophisticated CM tools to be used.

Key Points

- Every project has different CM requirements. Each project's approach to CM must be documented in its CM plan. The IEEE standard [IEEE-828 90] defines a structure for a CM plan.

- The CM plan must take account of many factors including the size of the project, the project's distribution, the use of third party software, the types of item to be managed, the project phase and whether variants are needed.

- The plan must itself be managed as an item. It evolves and is refined as the project progresses.

- Two rules to remember when evaluating CM tools are that the tool must meet the needs of the project (not vice versa) and that no CM tool is a panacea.

- Two aspects of CM which must be managed with particular care are the handover of software to a maintenance team and the introduction of good CM practices to a wayward project.

- There is a range of general standards, many not specific to CM or to software, which may be specialised to the CM requirements of a particular software project.

GLOSSARY

Archive   To archive is to move infrequently used data to a store which may be more expensive to access but is secure and cheap to maintain.

Backup   A copy of data made as insurance against loss or corruption.

Baseline *   An item which has been fully approved, serves as a basis for further development and can only be changed through formal change control procedures. Usually the term baseline refers to all items produced by a phase of the project lifecycle.

Build dependency   The dependency of a derived item upon the items from which it is derived.

Change control *   The process by which a change is proposed, evaluated, approved or rejected, scheduled and tracked.

Change control board, configuration control board, CCB *   The authority responsible for evaluating and approving or rejecting proposed changes and ensuring the implementation of approved changes.

Change request, CR   A request for a change to an item. A change request is recorded on a change request form, either paper or electronic, which also records the progress of the change request through its lifecycle.

Check in, Replace   To create a new version of an item in the software library. If the new version is not the first version of the item, the item is first checked out of the library.

---

* Indicates that the definition is as in [IEEE-729 83], either verbatim or in essence.

Check out, Reserve   To take a copy of a version of an item from the software library prior to modifying the item.

Configuration   See *Item*. Usually an item which is not a design item but fulfils a particular function.

Configuration audit *   The process of verifying that all items have been produced as specified and that change requests have been resolved.

Configuration management, CM *   The process of:

- Identifying and defining the items in a system (item identification).
- Controlling the release and change of these items (change control).
- Recording and reporting the status of these items (configuration status accounting).
- Verifying the completeness and correctness of items (configuration audit).

Configuration status accounting *   The recording and reporting of information needed for effective CM, including the status of all items and the status of all requests for change.

Dependent   An item X is dependent upon an item Y if a change to Y might require changes to X for X to remain correct. If X requires a compatible version of Y then X is dependent upon Y. The dependency of a derived element upon its source elements is called a build dependency.

Derived element   An element that is constructed by the automatic processing of other elements. An element that is not a derived element is a source element.

Design item   An item in the design hierarchy. Every element of the system is a leaf node of the design hierarchy and every design item, except the root of the hierarchy, has a unique parent.

Element   An item which does not decompose as smaller items.

Fault report, FR   A type of change request which reports a fault in an item.

Item, Configuration item, Configuration   Software which is treated as a unit for the purposes of CM. Formally the words item and configuration are synonymous. In practice the term configuration usually refers to a large composite item which performs a particular function.

Item identification, Configuration identification *   The process of designating the items in a system and recording their characteristics.

Release, Issue   The distribution of software outside the development organisation, for example to users.

Revision   One item version is a revision of another if it was created by modifying the earlier version which it supersedes. The set of all versions form a directed acyclic graph in which each version is connected to its revisions; branches in the graph correspond to item variants.

Source element   An element that is manually updated. An element which is not a source element is a derived element.

System model   A description of the items of the system and the relationships between them.

Version   An instance of an item. Where the context ensures there is no ambiguity, the unqualified term item may refer to an item version.

Variant   One item version is a variant of another if neither is a revision of the other. Variants allow one item to meet conflicting requirements at the same time: temporary variants allow parallel development and will eventually be merged; permanent variants are not merged but enable the item to meet different functional requirements.

REFERENCES

[ANSI 83] ANSI and AJPO, *Military Standard: Ada Programming Language*, ANSI/MIL-STD-1815A, 1983.

[Babich 86] Wayne A. Babich, *Software Configuration Management—Coordination for Team Productivity*, Addison-Wesley, New York, 1986.

[Bersoff 79] E. H. Bersoff, V.D. Henderson and S.G. Siegel, *Principles of Software Configuration Management*, Prentice-Hall, Englewood Cliffs, NJ, 1979.

[Bochm 81] Barry W. Boehm, *Software Engineering Economics*, Prentice-Hall, Englewood Cliffs, NJ, 1981.

[Boehm 86] Barry W. Boehm, A Spiral Model of Software Development and Enhancement, *ACM SIGSOFT Software Engineering Notes*, 11(4), 14–24 1986.

[Booch 87] Grady Booch, *Software Engineering with Ada*, Benjamin/Cummings, Redwood City, CA, 1987.

[Booch 91] Grady Booch, *Object Oriented Design with Applications*, Benjamin/ Cummings, Redwood City, CA, 1991.

[Brooks 75] Fred P. Brooks, *The Mythical Man Month*, Addison-Wesley, New York, 1975.

[Clemm 88] Geoffrey M. Clemm, The Odin Specification Language, *Proceedings of the International Workshop on Software Version and Configuration Control*, pp. 144–158, Teubner Verlag, Stuttgart, 1988.

[Cohen 86] Bernard Cohen, William T. Harwood and Mel I. Jackson, *The Specification of Complex Systems*, Addison-Wesley, New York, 1986.

[Constantine 79] Larry L. Constantine and Ed Yourdon, *Structured Design*, Prentice-Hall, Englewood Cliffs, NJ, 1979.

[Date 90] C. J. Date, *An Introduction to Database Systems*, 5th edition, Addison-Wesley, New York, 1990.

[Dijkstra 79]   E. Dijkstra, Programming considered as a human activity, *Classics in Software Engineering*, pp. 3–9, Yourdon Press, New York, 1979.

[DoD-2167A 88]   DoD 2167A, *Defence Systems Software Development*, DoD Naval Publications Center, Philadelphia, PA, 1988.

[DoD 85]   DoD 5200.28-STD, Department of Defence Trusted Computer System Evaluation Criteria, Office of Standards and Products, Maryland, 1985.

[Dowson 87]   Mark Dowson, Integrated Project Support with IStar, *IEEE Software*, 4(6), 6–15, 1987.

[Fagan 76]   M. E. Fagan, Design and Code Inspections to Reduce Errors in Program Development, *IBM Systems Journal*, 15(3), 182–211, 1976.

[Fagan 86]   M. E. Fagan, Advances in Software Inspections, *IEEE Transactions on Software Engineering*, **SE-12**(7), 744–751, 1986.

[Feldman 79]   Stuart I. Feldman, Make—A Program for Maintaining Computer Programs, *Software Practice and Experience*, 9(3), 255–265, March 1979.

[Goldfine 85]   Alan Goldfine and Patricia Konig, A Technical Overview of the Information Resource Dictionary System. *Computers and Standards*, 1, 153–208, 1985.

[Goos 83]   G. Goos and W.A. Wulf, *DIANA Reference Manual, Lecture Notes in Computer Science*, No 161, Springer-Verlag, New York, 1983.

[Hall 89]   Patrick A. V. Hall, Software Development Standards, *Software Engineering Journal*, 4(5), 143–147, May 1989.

[IBM 89]   *Systems Application Architecture: AD/Cycle Concepts*, GC26-4531-0, IBM Corporation, New York, 1989.

[IEEE-729 83]   ANSI/IEEE Std 729-1983, *Glossary of Software Engineering Terminology*, IEEE, New York, 1983.

[IEEE-828 90]   ANSI/IEEE Std 828-1990, *Standard for Software Configuration Management Plans*, IEEE, New York, 1990.

[IEEE-1042 87]   ANSI/IEEE Std 1042-1987, *Guide to Software Configuration Management*, IEEE, New York, 1987.

[ISO-9001 87]   ISO Standard 9001, *Quality Systems: Assurance of Design/Development, Production, Installation and Servicing Capability*, International Standards Organisation, Switzerland, 1987.

[Kernighan 78]   Brian W. Kernighan and Dennis M. Ritchie, *The C Programming Language*, Prentice-Hall, Englewood Cliffs, NJ, 1978.

[Knudsen 77]   D. B. Knudsen, A. Barofsky and L. R. Satz, A Modification Request Control System, *Proceedings of the 2nd International Conference on Software Engineering*, pp. 187–192, IEEE and ACM, New York, 1977.

[Knuth 73]   D. E. Knuth, *The Art of Computer Programming*, Volume 3 (*Sorting and Searching*), Addison-Wesley, New York, 1973.

[Kruskal 84]   V. Kruskal, Managing Multi-version Programs with an Editor, *IBM Journal of Research and Development*, **28**(1), 74–81, 1984.

[Lampson 83]   Bruce W. Lampson and Eric E. Schmidt, Organising Software in a Distributed Environment, *Proceedings of the SIGPLAN 83 Symposium on Programming Language Issues in Software Systems*, San Francisco, Calif., 1983.

[Leblang 87]   David B. Leblang and Robert P. Chase, Parallel Software Configuration Management in a Network Environment, *IEEE Software*, **4**(6), 28–35, November 1987.

[Leblang 88]   David B. Leblang, Robert P. Chase and Howard Spilke, Increasing Productivity with a Parallel Configuration Manager, *Proceedings of the International Workshop on Software Version and Configuration Control*, pp. 21–37, Teubner Verlag, Stuttgart, 1988.

[Meyers 79]   G. J. Meyers, *The Art of Software Testing*, John Wiley, New York, 1979.

[Montes 88]   Juan Montes and Tani Haque, A Configuration Management System and More! *Proceedings of the International Workshop on Software Version and Configuration Control*, pp. 217–227, Teubner Verlag, Stuttgart, 1988.

[OU 87]   *Project Management (PMT 605): Change Control*, Open University Press, Milton Keynes, 1987.

[Ould 90]   Martyn A. Ould, *Managing Software Engineering—The Management of Risk and Quality*, John Wiley, Chichester, 1990.

[Parnas 72]   David Parnas, On the Criteria to be Used in Decomposing Systems into Modules, *Communications of the ACM*, **15**(2), 1053–1058, 1972.

[PCTE 88]   *PCTE+ Ada and C Functional Specifications*, Issue 3, GIE Emeraude, Paris, 1988.

[QAS 87]   *Quality Assurance Schedule to ISO 9001 for Use with Electronic Computer Systems Equipment*, BSI, Milton Keynes, 1987.

[Reps 88]   Thomas Reps, Susan Horwitz and Jan Prins, Support for Integrating Program Variants in an Environment for Programming in the Large, *Proceedings of the International Workshop on Software Version and Configuration Control*, pp. 197–216, Teubner Verlag, Stuttgart, 1988.

[Rochkind 75]   Marc J. Rochkind, The Source Code Control System, *IEEE Transactions on Software Engineering*, **SE-1**(4), 364–370, December 1975.

[Royce 70]   W. W. Royce, Managing the Development of Large Software Systems: Concepts and Techniques, *Proceedings of Wescon*, 1970.

[Sarnak 88]   N. Sarnak, R. Bernstein and V. Kruskal, Creation and Maintenance of Multiple Versions, *Proceedings of the International Workshop on Software Version and Configuration Control*, pp. 264–275, Teubner Verlag, Stuttgart, 1988.

[Sommerville 89]   Ian Sommerville, *Software Engineering*, 3rd edition, Addison-Wesley, New York, 1989.

[Tichy 85]   Walter F. Tichy, RCS—A System for Version Control, *Software—Practice and Experience*, 15(7), 637–654, July 1985.

[Tichy 86]   Walter F. Tichy, Smart Recompilation, *ACM Transactions on Programming Languages and Systems*, 8(3), 273–291, July 1986.

[Tichy 88]   Walter F. Tichy, Tools for Software Configuration Management, *Proceedings of the International Workshop on Software Version and Configuration Control*, pp. 1–20 Teubner Verlag, Stuttgart, 1988.

[Winkler 88]   Jurgen F. H. Winkler and Clemens Stoffel, Program-Variations-in-the-Small, *Proceedings of the International Workshop on Software Version and Configuration Control*, pp. 175–196, Teubner Verlag, Stuttgart, 1988.

[Youll 90]   David P. Youll, *Making Software Engineering Visible—Effective Project Control*, John Wiley, Chichester, 1990.

COMMERCIAL CONFIGURATION MANAGEMENT TOOLS

To illustrate how software tools help to provide effective CM, this book describes several commercially available CM tools. The objective is not to describe any tool completely, or to describe the complete product line of the tool's supplier, or to survey all CM tools, or select the best CM tool. Further details of the following tools can be obtained from the tool's supplier.

CMS® (Code Management System) and *MMS*® (Module Management System) are registered trademarks of
Digital Equipment Corporation
Maynard, Massachusetts
CMS and MMS run on a VAX/VMS platform.

CCC® (Change and Configuration Control)
is a registered trademark of
Softool Corporation
340 South Kellogg Avenue, Goleta, California 93117
CCC runs on VAX, IBM and a range of Unix platforms.

DSEE® (Domain Software Engineering Environment)
is a registered trademark of
Hewlett-Packard Apollo
Chelmsford, Massachusetts
DSEE runs on HP Apollo workstations.

Lifespan®
is a registered trademark of
Yard Software Systems Ltd, part of Sema Group plc
Avonbridge House, Bath Road, Chippenham, Wiltshire SN15 2BB
Lifespan runs on a VAX/VMS platform.

PCMS® (Product Change Management System)
is a registered trademark of
SQL Systems Ltd
Latton Bush Centre, Southern Way, Harlow, Essex CM18 7BL
PCMS runs on VAX/VMS and a range of Unix platforms.

Rational® and *Rational Environment*®
are registered trademarks of
Rational
3320 Scott Boulevard, Santa Clara, California 95064
Rational runs on its own purpose designed platform.

The following are also trademarks:

Ada® is a registered trademark of the US Government.
VAX® and *VMS*® are registered trademarks of Digital Equipment
Corporation.

INDEX